Go for Me to China

Originally published as: *Ga voor Mij naar China – Leven en werk van Hudson Taylor*
Author: J. Kranendonk-Gijssen
Publisher: B.V. Uitgeverij De Banier, 2013
Illustrations: Jack Staller

Go for Me to China – The Life and Work of Hudson Taylor
Cover design: Albert Bloemert – Rebecca Lyn
Translation: Frank Westerink
Typesetting: Architype Graphic Solutions
ISBN 978-1-62847-466-4

© Hudson Taylor Ministries – www.hudsontaylor.us

All profit from this publication will be used to support the work of Hudson Taylor Ministries. All rights reserved.

Printed in the USA

The Life and Work of Hudson Taylor

Go for Me to China

J. Kranendonk-Gijssen

Contents

1. A Nice Saturday	9
2. To School and to the Bank	14
3. God Answers Prayer	19
4. Called to China	24
5. The Lord Cares	28
6. Assistant in Hull	31
7. Trusting in God Alone	36
8. Money Worries Again	40
9. The Hospital in London	44
10. In Danger of Life	49
11. Exciting Development in China	53
12. The Voyage	57
13. A Long Journey	63
14. Arrival in Shanghai	68
15. The Gospel in the Interior Also	72
16. A True Chinese	77
17. A New Friend	83
18. Working in Ningbo	89
19. Joy and Sorrow	94
20. A God of Miracles	99
21. Back to England	103
22. Praying and Working for China	107
23. Back to China	115
24. A Deep Trial	119
25. The Eleventh and Last Trip	122
From the Author	127
Hudson Taylor's Life	128
Important People in this Book	131

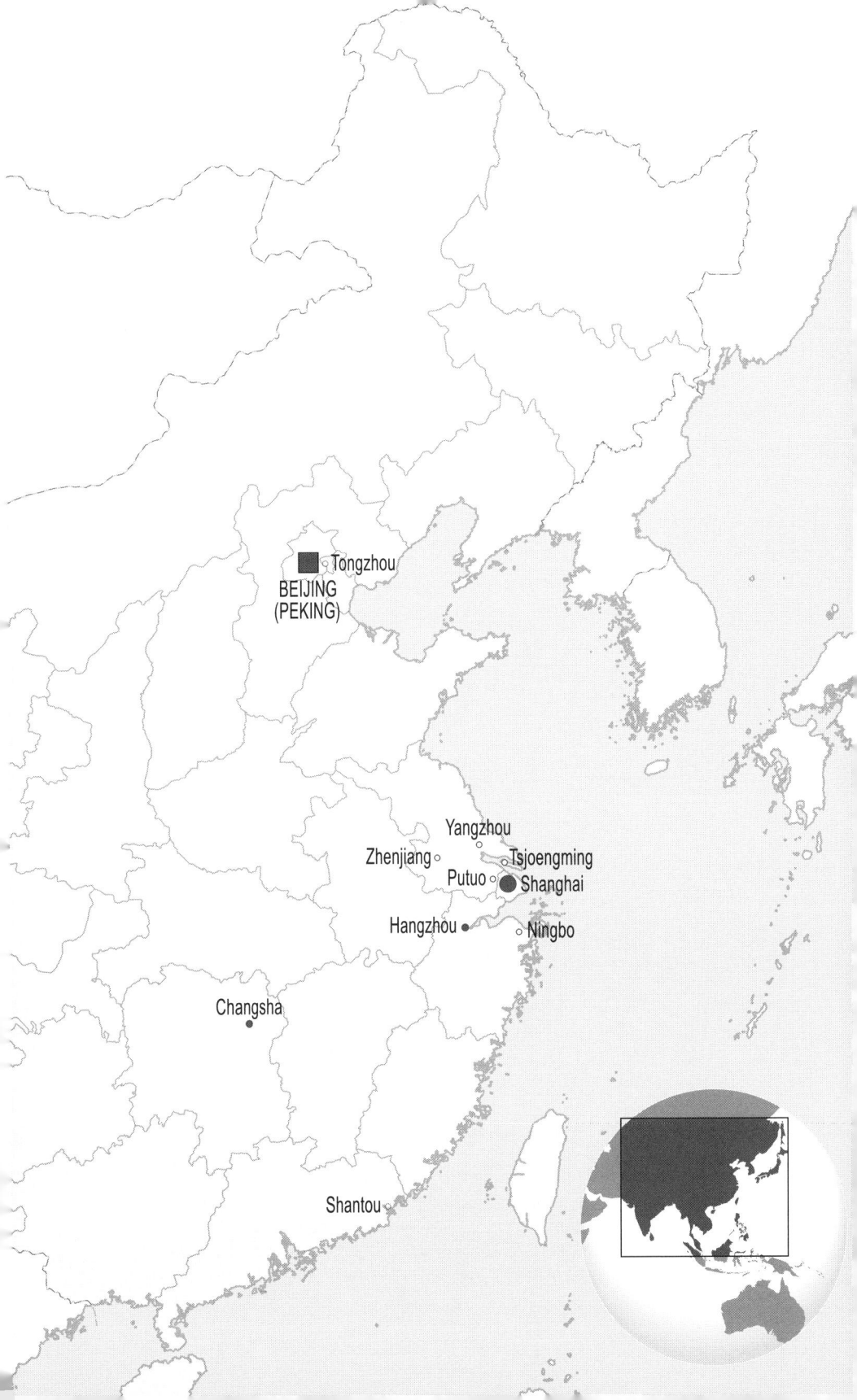

1. A Nice Saturday

1841

"Watch out! Get out of the way, Amelia!" Panting, Hudson Taylor ran after his hoop with a beaming face as he rolled it down the hill. He was having fun! The hoop was moving so fast that he could hardly keep up.

In amazement Amelia looked at her brother who was three years older than her. She just could not understand it. Her hoop kept falling over, no matter what she tried. And Hudson's kept rolling down, as straight as an arrow.

"Just wait," her father smiled. "Soon you will be running as fast as Hudson, Amelia. You'll do fine once you catch on. Just keep on trying and don't give up." Amelia gathered up all her courage and tried once more.

With big steps Father Taylor tried to keep up with his two children. It had been very busy at the pharmacy during the past week. He was happy to leave all the hustle and bustle of the city behind him. On Saturday afternoon the children usually spent their time outdoors and he came along whenever he could.

Oh, Hudson had been very impatient that afternoon; he could hardly wait.

Father Hudson's eyes sparkled as he quickly scanned Hudson's magazine about nature. It had to come along, although playing hoops with a magazine in your hand did not really work. Well, he could understand. He also used to enjoy learning about birds, flowers, plants and insects. Hudson certainly did not inherit his love of nature from a stranger.

* * *

A short while later a red-faced Hudson waited for his father and sister at the edge of the forest. He was panting.

"That wasn't very smart," Father said. "You've tired yourself out. You have only just recuperated. Let's take it easy for the rest of the afternoon. Be careful, because otherwise I will have to prepare a special medicine for you tonight."

Hudson nodded obediently. "But can I ... the magazine, Father? This afternoon ... aren't we going to ... look for different kinds of ferns?"

"Yes certainly, but, as I said, just take it easy. You can hardly talk. Let's sit down on this tree stump here. Then we'll decide which types of ferns we should look for."

"May I have my pill box, Father?" Amelia asked impatiently. "Then I can look for beetles." She was happy that they were finally in the forest. Looking for beetles was much more fun than playing with hoops, especially now that she had received such a nice little box from Father to put the insects in.

It was not long before the children were busy looking around.

"Look here; this is a special kind of fern!" Hudson called out enthusiastically.

"Shh, be quiet," Amelia warned, "otherwise all the beetles will disappear!"

Hudson ducked behind a thick tree. He almost burst out laughing, but he did not want Amelia to see him laughing at her. But William would never have done something like that ...

Alarmed, Hudson put his hand in front of his mouth. William ... It was about a year and a half ago that he had died. William had been seven years old, only two years younger than him. William had not only been his younger brother, but also his best friend. Now there were only three children in the family: Amelia, little Louisa and he.

A dark shadow covered Hudson's face. Suddenly it seemed as if the Saturday afternoon was not so enjoyable anymore. William would never come along with them again.

* * *

"Man, why does someone have to knock on the pharmacy door tonight? Can Father not have one night off? We've been waiting for him for fifteen minutes already," Hudson complained, as he walked to the big window in the living room which overlooked the market square of the city of Barnsley.

He had been looking forward to this evening. On Saturday night Father always told his children exciting stories. He knew a lot about history and he had promised that he would ask them all kinds of questions about China. During the past week, Amelia and he had done their utmost to find out new things about China in Father's extensive library.

"Be quiet, Hudson," Mother warned. "It's true that your father is very busy but you also know that he enjoys helping people. Maybe he's helping a poor man who heard that Father does not send a bill to people who cannot afford to pay him. The Lord Jesus asks us to love others."

Hudson pressed his nose against the cold window. He knew Mother was right.

"Come, you can help me," Mother said softly. "Let's make tea and prepare something good to eat."

"Hmm ... something good to eat!" Amelia immediately jumped off her chair and ran to the kitchen.

They were just finished when Father entered the living room.

"Well, here I am, children. Is everything ready? Good! Let's go and sit on the couch together."

He didn't say anything about the patient who had interrupted his Saturday evening.

"Remind me. What were we going to do tonight?"

"Ask questions about China, Father!"

"Yes, that's right. Okay, let's start with a question for Amelia. Let me think. Which country has the largest number of people?"

"China," she said proudly.

"That's correct. Now I have a question for you, Hudson. What is a dialect that has the same name as a certain type of fruit?"

Hudson hesitated for a minute and then he said resolutely, "The Mandarin dialect, Father."

"That's also correct. I have another question for you, Amelia. What food is most popular in China?"

"Rice!"

"Good. Hudson, another question about fruit for you. What's the name of the leader of a village or city in China?"

"A Mandarin."

"Amelia, what awful thing is done to the girls in China?"

"Their feet are always bound up very tightly so that they don't become very big. And, um ... that's why the girls have a lot of trouble walking."

'Hudson, name the three most important discoveries of the Chinese."

"They invented gun powder, the compass and book printing."

'Correct. Amelia, who discovered paper?"

"Ha ha," she laughed, "also the Chinese. Do you know how I know that? Hudson read that to me yesterday."

"That's very smart of you," Mother said as she winked at her children. She was observing the threesome from her rocking chair. "You know quite a bit about China."

Suddenly Hudson frowned. He put his hand on his father's knee and said, "Do you know what I cannot understand, Father? That there are still no missionaries in China. I looked everywhere in your books about China but I could not find anything about that. That's why I often pray that I may become a missionary in China when I am older."

Father and Mother Hudson looked at each other knowingly. They were both thinking the same thing. That was also their greatest wish. But they wondered if it would ever happen because Hudson was often sick.

"And I want to come along too," Amelia said forcefully. "Hudson and I agreed to that when he read to me from Peter Parley's book about China. Right, Hudson?"

"I think it is time for the children to go to bed, Father," Mother observed. "Look at Amelia. She cannot even keep her eyes open."

Hudson and Amelia were tired but they were also happy that they had such a nice day. They said goodnight to their parents.

"May we have a quick look at Louisa?" Hudson asked.

"If you're very quiet," Mother said.

The children and Father tiptoed to the cradle where their little sister was sleeping. Then they knelt down by Father and Mother's big bed.

After the children respectfully folded their hands, Father put his big arms around them, as he did every evening.

Together they thanked the Lord for everything which He had given them that day. After Father asked the Lord to take care of them during the night, he prayed, "Lord, Wilt Thou grant that someday there will be missionaries who will go to China to tell the people that Thou hast sent Thy Son to this earth to save sinners?"

"Thank you, Father," Hudson whispered, "that we also prayed for the people in China."

2. To School and to the Bank

1843-1849

Hudson turned over restlessly. Phew! He felt warm in his bed. He had been tossing and turning for more than an hour. He was very excited because tomorrow he would be going to school for the first time, even though he was already eleven years old. Because he was often sick, his parents had decided that he should be home-schooled until now.

When he went to bed that night, Father had said that he should not worry too much. He had been able to read already when he was only four. Actually, at that age he even knew the Hebrew alphabet by heart. Not everyone could do that. For years he had finished difficult language lessons with Mother and math exercises with Father. He wondered if his new teacher would be as strict as his father. He hoped not.

Thankfully Mother had told him that afternoon that everything would turn out all right at his new school. She always understood him well.

Hudson turned over another time. What would the classroom look like? It was probably a lot different from their living room where he had always done his homework. It was nice and cozy. Every afternoon Mother sat in her rocking chair at the table to check his work. He would certainly miss that. He also wondered what the other boys would be like. Would they like him or maybe not?

Hudson stared into the darkness with big eyes. He tried not to think of the next day. He wished everything could stay the way it was. Maybe he should imagine that he was going on a trip to China. He had just checked the world atlas that evening. He thought of all the countries he would pass and all the seas and rivers he would cross to finally reach Shanghai with his sailboat.

He squeezed his eyes shut tightly and pretended he was sailing the Atlantic Ocean. It would be very nice if he could travel to China someday!

* * *

It was just over two years later. Hudson was standing in the pharmacy dressed in his nice white coat, waiting for his father. Father had taken a customer into the living room to discuss some medical concerns with him. Hudson was very proud of his father. Sometimes he looked just like a doctor. Hudson wanted to be as smart as his father when he grew up. That's why he studied Father's medical books for awhile every day, although he did not understand everything he read.

Today he was allowed to mix medicines for the first time. When he had started working at the pharmacy just after Christmas, he had only been allowed to package the medicines. After that he was allowed to weigh them. The job was becoming more and more difficult. He had to pay very close attention, especially when he was mixing different substances. Imagine if he would prepare the wrong medicine!

His eyes scanned the glass jars with the beautiful labels. He felt like a fish in the water in his father's pharmacy. He was happy that he did not need to go to school every day. He had enjoyed the contact with the other boys but he had actually not learned very much during the two years at school. And because he was now thirteen, he had to earn some money.

There was one incident from his years at school that he could not forget. It was the afternoon when a speaker by the name of Henry Reed had been invited to the school. He had told the students about his experiences in Tasmania.

Hudson felt a small shiver go down his back. He wished he could forget the whole incident but he kept thinking about the story. Mr. Reed had told them about a man who had committed a murder even though he knew very well that it was a crime. The last night, before his execution, he heard the voice of the Lord, which said to him, "My son, give me thine heart." Whenever Hudson thought of this text, his heart began to beat faster, just as it had when he heard Mr. Reed tell the story. It was as if the Lord said this to him. And he felt anxious whenever he thought of the text. He would rather not listen to this inner voice. He did not pray as earnestly now as he used to. His prayers kept getting shorter and shorter and he hardly ever read his Bible when he was in his room. He had more and more doubts about whether everything that he had been taught was true. Why should he not be allowed to enjoy the things of this world? Was it true what his father said from the pulpit every Sunday, when he led the service in their small congregation? Would it not be better if Father were only a pharmacist?

Deep in his heart, Hudson felt that he would really like to become rich. He did not like it when Father and Mother warned him against all kinds of things, which he did secretly sometimes. He never told his parents but he wondered sometimes if Mother knew everything he did. Occasionally, it seemed as if she was looking right through him. He always hoped she would not ask any questions! He did not want to cause his mother any sorrow. Suddenly he was startled from his sombre thoughts. The store bell rang and a new customer entered. Hudson was happy that he had something else to think about.

* * *

"Well, you might think that the people in your church are always right, but how can you be sure? Why would God only tell you what He wants?" Hudson Taylor's colleague laughed scornfully as he walked back to his desk.

Seventeen-year-old Hudson felt defeated as he stood by the coat rack of the Bank of Barnsley. He didn't know what to say. Before this, he had looked forward to working as a junior administrator at the bank for awhile. The plan was that in this way he would learn about administration and business communication. And it was true that the bank was much better suited for that than the pharmacy. But he had not expected that he would receive so much criticism as a Christian.

Hudson buttoned up his coat, put on his scarf and walked home. He felt sad. Not a day passed that he didn't hear mocking comments. One colleague had said to him recently, "You Christians are all hypocrites. You say that you believe in the Bible, right? But when I look at

how you live, do you know what I sometimes think? It seems as if you have never read the Bible!"

Deep in his heart, he had to agree with this colleague. At least … when he looked into his own heart. What did he actually still believe? He could not imagine that as a child he always simply believed what Father and Mother told him. He did not pray or read his Bible at all anymore. He even felt irritated when Father read aloud from the Bible after breakfast. And even more when he prayed for another twenty minutes after that. It all took far too long. Imagine if it were true what his colleague had said, that there was no life after this life. Why should he then lead such a pious life instead of enjoying himself? Who could prove to him that God really existed?

As he turned the corner, he saw his parents' house in the distance.

Another difficulty was that he could not really talk to his father about these things. He had tried several times but each time they had ended up having a fierce argument. He did not talk to Father very often anymore. He still talked to Mother sometimes but he did not really tell her the secrets of his heart any longer. She sometimes squeezed his shoulder or just looked at him. Did she understand how many questions he had and how much doubt there was in his heart?

He was happy that he still had Amelia. Occasionally he told her about his troubles. She could not answer all his questions but still … she was always willing to listen to him.

3. God Answers Prayer

1849

Which book should he read this afternoon? Hudson Taylor was standing in front of his father's enormous bookcase. It was a beautiful summer day in June, but he did not feel like going outside because it was too hot in the city. He did not really know what to do on his afternoon off. It was very quiet in the house because Mother was staying with her sister for a few days and Father was busy in the pharmacy.

His eyes slowly scanned the long rows of books. He knew the contents of most of them. Without thinking he took a basket with tracts and turned it upside down. Maybe there was something he could read. He did not feel like reading a religious book. That time was past.

He picked a small tract out of the pile. It was published by an evangelical committee. He quickly leafed through it: a story and a sermon. Well, he was not going to read the sermon but the story looked sort of interesting. He put the other tracts back in the basket and took the tract along as he walked to the barn in the garden. It was nice and cool there because of the shadow from the big chestnut tree. This was his favourite spot, where he would be able to read without being interrupted.

Soon he was captivated by the story. It was about a miner who was seriously ill. He had tuberculosis. All signs pointed to an imminent death. Several Christians visited the man and read to him from the Bible. And … that message touched his heart, especially the part where Jesus called out on the cross, "It is finished!" The sick miner confessed his sins, believed in the Lord Jesus and became a Christian.

Shocked, Hudson dropped the tract. Suddenly it was as if he saw the last few years of his life pass by him. He felt alone with God in the barn. He knew for certain that what this tract said was true. Oh, how could he ever have been preoccupied with all the comments of his colleagues at the bank? How could he have doubted the existence of God? How had he dared to doubt the message of God?

It was as if he felt a terrible pain deep inside. What had he done? The last few years he had distanced himself more and more from God. He was a far greater sinner than the miner. That man had never heard of God, whereas he had tried very consciously not to think about God. He had done what the Bible called "resisting the Holy Spirit". He felt that he would never be able to reconcile himself with God. Only the Lord Jesus, who died for sinners, could save him.

Suddenly everything was different in his heart. He was no longer angry with God. Instead, he longed for Him! In amazement Hudson Taylor fell on to his knees and called out, "Oh Lord, there is salvation with Thee. Thou hast accomplished everything. I can only kneel before Thee, who hast looked for people who are only sin and who have sin. How great is Thy love!"

As he lay on his knees, a marvellous peace entered his heart. He felt that Jesus also wanted to forgive his sins by the power of the Holy Spirit!

* * *

That same afternoon a tired Mother Taylor wiped the sweat off her forehead. It was hot. She had just cleaned up the table and told her sister Hannah that she would like to spend the afternoon in her room by herself. But it was not only the heat which was bothering her. It was as if she had a stone in her stomach.

Carefully she locked the door of the guest room behind her. She was very worried about Hudson. She kept thinking about him, even though she was away from home. She had not slept at all during the night because she kept on agonizing about her son. Why had he changed so much? She and her husband had prayed so often for their child, and yet he had distanced himself more and more from God and matters of faith during the last few years. A sob welled up in her throat. She loved her son so much and she could not understand this. She had always hoped that Hudson would labour in God's Kingdom as an adult. And now? He did not even want to go to church anymore.

Tears ran down her cheeks. Everything used to be so different. Hudson often read the Bible by himself, also in the evening when he was in bed. Her thoughts wandered back in time. One evening they had received visitors. Hudson had been allowed to stay up for awhile to have something to drink. He had several end pieces of candles in his pants pocket, because he had wanted to read his Bible in bed for a long time. One of the guests who was seated close to the fireplace had put Hudson on her lap and the pieces of candle had melted in his pocket. Then she had been angry with him but now she wished that he would read a good book or that he would take the Bible out of the cupboard. Oh, she would give everything to see that happen. Actually, he had changed from the time that he was about twelve years old. And since he had started to work at the bank it had only become worse. What would the future hold for him?

She felt that neither she nor her husband could solve this problem; only the Lord could help.

Reverently she knelt down and told all her troubles to the Lord. She resolved not to get up before she knew that the Lord had heard her prayer.

She prayed and begged for several hours in a row. Until … she felt she could pray no longer, but that she had to give thanks! Then she could firmly believe that God had answered her prayer.

* * *

"Amelia, can I tell you a secret?"

"Of course, Hudson. You know you can tell me anything." Amelia looked at her big brother affectionately. He didn't know that she wrote about him in her daily diary and that she prayed for him every day, asking God to protect him. She loved Hudson very much. A few years ago they had agreed that they would go to China together when they were old enough. She wondered whether that would ever happen.

"Amelia," Hudson began. He hesitated and sat down beside her. "A few days ago a great miracle happened. You know that I have tried to forget God. I wanted to live as if there is no life after this life. But God was stronger than I."

Reverently Hudson told his sister how he had been reading the evangelical tract in the barn and how the words "It is finished" changed his life.

With tears in her eyes, Amelia listened to his story. She was so happy that the Lord had heard her prayers!

"How amazing, Hudson," she said softly. "Think of how happy Father and Mother will be ..."

"Shh," Hudson interrupted her. "We're not going to say anything to Father. I'm going to tell them once Mother is home."

"Sure," Amelia nodded, as she shook hands with Hudson. "I promise I won't tell anyone."

* * *

That day was a special day. Louisa and Amelia Taylor were standing by the window. They could hardly wait. Mother's carriage would arrive any moment. She had only been gone for two weeks, but it seemed like it had been much longer. The two sisters had big news!

In the pharmacy Father and Hudson Taylor also found it difficult to concentrate on their work. Hudson especially kept looking through the window. How surprised Mother would be with his wonderful message. He knew very well that he had caused her much grief. He wanted to ask for her, and Father's, forgiveness.

The noise of the carriage turning onto the market square startled him. Mother was home!

With big steps he walked through the door towards the carriage, even before it had stopped in front of the house.

"Mother," he sobbed as he hugged her. "I have good news for you." Mother pulled him even closer against her and said with a voice full of emotion, "I know already, my boy. I have been extremely happy about the good news since last week."

In total surprise Hudson looked at his mother. "Mother, but ... how do you know? Did Amelia tell you after all?"

"Oh no, my boy. I have not even talked to Amelia yet. How could I talk to her? No one has talked to me about you, but the Lord has told me what has happened to you. Come, let's go inside. Then I'll explain it all to you."

Once they were all seated in the living room, Mother told them of the great miracle that she had experienced one afternoon in the past week. The suitcases were still standing unopened in the hallway, but no one noticed. Even little Louisa felt that something special was happening, although she could not understand how it was possible that Mother had been so far away and yet she had known what had happened here at home. She didn't know what to think.

After Mother had told her story, it was Hudson's turn. Deeply moved the others listened to him.

After a short silence Father stood up and said, "I propose that we thank the Lord together for bringing Mother back home safely and for the great miracle that He has performed!"

4. Called to China

1849

Hudson Taylor was sitting in front of his writing table with his hands supporting his head. It was Sunday morning. Father, Mother and Louisa had gone to church but he had such a bad cold that he could not go along. It was noisy outside but Hudson did not notice the clanging bells of the carriages, which were driving to and from the market square. He also did not notice the whirling snowflakes which coloured the street white. Hudson was deep in thought.

Much had happened during the past six months. Actually, everything had changed. Before, he had been an enemy of God. However, after he had been enabled to behold the Lord Jesus, who cried out "It is finished", his greatest desire had become the service of the Lord.

Thankfulness filled his heart. Since that special moment in June, he not only felt reconciled with God but also with his family, and especially with his father. And his bond with his sister Amelia had become even stronger. For a few months they had even spent their Sunday evenings going to poor areas of the city to distribute evangelical tracts. Sometimes they had told the people about the riches of faith.

His hand moved through his thick curls. He wondered how Amelia was doing. He missed her every day. In September, she had gone to Aunt Hannah in Barton-upon-Humber to get an education at a boarding school. He wished that his mother's sister had never made this proposal. What was worse, Aunt Hannah's oldest son John was now staying at their house. During the day he studied and worked at the pharmacy, but at night he slept in Hudson's room. In short, his cousin John was in his vicinity twenty-four hours a day.

When Hudson thought back to the nice time just after his conversion, he felt sad. Then he sometimes read the Bible until late at night. But ever since he had to share his room with John, he did not have the opportunity for that. The one time John joked about faith and another time he mocked the church or he wanted the oil lamp put out so he could sleep. It was just one problem after another.

Hudson sighed.

Yet there were not only negative things. The Lord had also given him courage. Just when he had to complain like the Apostle Paul: "For the good that I would I do not: but the evil which I would not, that I do", he read an article in a magazine about "Living holily for the Lord". It had touched him deeply. That's how he wanted to live: only for the Lord! Occasionally he was afraid that he would live without God again, just like he had done before his conversion. But through that article, his heart was set on fire again. The Lord was everything for him!

He wished that Amelia were home. Then he could tell her everything. But wait ... he could write her a letter! He took a crown pen out of the holder, opened the ink pot and began to write:

Barnsley, December 2, 1840

Dear Amelia,

Are things going well in Barton-upon-Humber? Thank God that He found me. That He loves me. Because in my heart I feel that I am not worthy of His blessings. I give in so easily to wicked things. I like to have pleasure and love to tease. Will you please pray for me, Amelia? I would very much like to live a holy life before the Lord. On Sunday at church Mr. Simons gave me a card with the text: "Then will I sprinkle clean water upon you, and ye shall be clean." Oh, I would love to live completely holy before God. I have done everything to forget God, but He still wanted to forgive my sins. Therefore, I will never be able to love Him enough.

Today I could not go to church because I have quite a bad cold. Do you know what I wish? That I could go to heaven now. Sometimes I have such a great desire to die. Then I shall be with Christ forever. That is much better! Pray for me, Amelia!

* * *

That Sunday Hudson stayed inside for the whole day.

"Go to bed on time," his mother said at the end of the day. "Maybe you'll feel better tomorrow."

"You're right, Mother," Hudson said absentmindedly. He did not know why, but he longed very much to be alone in his room. What he longed for most was to tell God everything that was living in his heart. He was happy that his cousin John was not home so he could be alone with the Lord.

As soon as he reached his room, he knelt in front of his bed. He could no longer wait. Fervently he prayed, "Lord, If Thou wilt break the power of sin in my heart and if Thou wilt save me for time and eternity, then I will give up everything. Then I will dedicate my whole life unto Thee from now on. Then I will go wherever Thou sendest me. Then I am even willing to suffer for Thee."

A holy reverence filled his heart. He felt that the Lord was very close to him. He knew for certain that God had heard his prayer.

Suddenly, it was as if he heard a voice which said to him, "Go for Me to China. I have appeared to you to appoint you as My servant. You will be a witness of the things which you have seen and of the things in which I, the Lord, will appear unto you. I am sending you to open the eyes of the heathens, that they may come out of their darkness and to the Light. I am sending you that they may be delivered from the power of Satan, and come to Me, the God of heaven and earth."

Hudson felt that this was a holy moment! The Lord had given him a personal message. He could hardly believe it! Momentarily, he was speechless, but then he cried with joy, "Bless the Lord, O my soul: and all that is within me, bless His holy name!"

* * *

It was very quiet in the Taylor home. The only light still burning was in Hudson's room. It was night, but Hudson could not sleep. The Lord had given him a task. He now knew for sure that he would go to China. Even if he would have to suffer for the Name of the Lord Jesus, all was well.

How would this all happen? He did not know. But if God had called him, He would also take care of everything. What a wonder that he was allowed to be His witness among millions of people, among people who had never heard of Christ.

Again he longed to see Amelia. The envelope with the letter he had written that morning was still on the writing table. He decided to add something to the letter and then mail it the next day.

He did not hesitate any longer but got out of bed. He walked to the writing table as quietly as possible. Carefully he opened the envelope and read what he had written that morning. He did not feel cold. He had only one desire: to tell Amelia what the Lord had told him. He picked up the crown pen again and held his breath as he wrote:

Amelia, I want to tell you something else. The Lord spoke to me tonight. The Lord Jesus has said, "Seek and ye shall find." And God allows Himself to be found. This evening He gave me a task, namely, "Go for Me to China." I can hardly write for joy. Glory be to the Name of God. Goodbye Amelia.

5. The Lord Cares

1850

It was still early in the morning. Hudson had just started the fireplace and the orange-red flames danced among the blocks of wood. The windows were still frozen. Hudson and his cousin John were sitting at the table in the living room by the light of a smoky oil lamp. They each had a Bible in front of them, and a book with Chinese characters lay between them.

Hudson was excited. Today he was starting his study of Chinese! He had started getting up at five o'clock every morning to study Latin, Greek, Hebrew and Algebra. Now that he was certain he would be going to China, he wanted to prepare himself as well as he possibly could for his further work.

When he had obtained a copy of the gospel of Luke in the Chinese-Mandarin dialect the evening before, his cousin John had put forward an excellent proposal. He wanted to study together with Hudson so he could learn more about the Bible.

A miracle had also happened in John's life. In the past, John had often mocked Hudson when he wanted to read the Bible or pray before going to bed. But everything had changed. John also wanted to serve the Lord now. God was indeed at work in Barnsley.

"John," Hudson said as he leafed through the Bible, "let's compare how the word 'fear' has been translated into Chinese. For instance, Luke wrote in chapter 1 verse 30: 'And the angel said unto her, Fear not, Mary.' Is that the same word for fear as in the text: 'And fear came on all that dwelt round about them?' If the Chinese symbols are the same, then we will write the word in ink in this notebook. And we'll write the meaning behind it in pencil. Do you think that's a good idea?"

"Very good, Hudson! Then we can make a whole list of words which you can use to explain things once you're in China."

"I certainly hope so!" Hudson sighed. "I also hope that before that time I will meet someone who can teach me the pronunciation of the words. But we have to start somewhere."

The young men studied the Chinese characters intently. It was not easy because some of them were very similar.

"It is a very painstaking job, John. It will be some time before we can write a complete sentence!"

* * *

With a friendly smile the mailman handed a letter to Mother Taylor. As soon as she read who had sent it, her heart began to beat faster. It was a letter from Aunt Hannah from Hull. Would it be a positive message? Would there be a place for Hudson?

She hurried to the living room to open the letter. Her eyes flew across the sentences.

It was possible! Oh, she hardly dared to believe it.

She hesitated for a minute. She could not really walk into the pharmacy for a private message, but she could not wait either. Hudson and her husband had to know!

She pulled the curtain aside a little bit and checked if there were any people in the store. No, it was empty. She could no longer contain herself.

"Father, Hudson!" she called with a beaming face, as she walked into the pharmacy.

"Listen. I just received a letter from Aunt Hannah from Hull and do you know what it says? Her husband's brother, the well-known surgeon Robert Hardey, has an opening for an assistant!"

Hudson stared at his mother in utter amazement. Was … was this an answer to prayer? He had asked the Lord very earnestly if He would find a solution, and now Mother had received this letter!

He blushed.

"Mother, is this the same surgeon who has a large practice, and who is the supervising surgeon in several factories and who is also a teaching surgeon at the medical school in Hull?"

"Yes, that's him!"

"But … then I know for sure. The Lord has given a solution."

"Indeed, Hudson." Father nodded. "I believe you're right. I am happy and thankful about this. I cannot teach you much more here in the pharmacy. It would be wise for you to begin a medical study, especially if you ever want to go to China."

6. Assistant in Hull

1851-1852

In a steady rhythm the train rambled through the hilly landscape of Yorkshire. Hudson Taylor could not believe his eyes. He had never made such a far journey and certainly not alone. His suitcase was standing next to him on the wooden bench. He had planned to do some reading on the long trip, but he did not want to miss any of the beautiful landscapes which he was passing through.

It was a very special Monday. He had turned nineteen today but he was not celebrating his birthday at home. Today he would be starting his new job with Doctor Hardey in Hull. He wondered if he would be able to find his house quickly. He had a little piece of paper in his coat pocket which said *3 Charlotte Street.* That was the street where almost all the doctors of Hull had their practices. He was sure he would be able to find the house, especially if he used Aunt Hannah's directions.

It had not been easy to say goodbye to his family. Especially Mother had found it difficult. They both knew that the big farewell, for his departure to China, was coming closer and closer. Compared to that, this morning's farewell had been easier. He had wondered more often if he would ever see his parents again once he left for China. But Mother had tried hard to compose herself this morning. She had said, "Hudson, it is a joy and a privilege to suffer for the Name of the Lord Jesus. Therefore I want to put all my trust in God, also now that you are going to Hull."

Mother's words had also made it easier for him to say goodbye. He knew he would miss his family during the coming months. But he was certain that God, who had given him this job in a miraculous way, would also take care of him in the future. He wanted to follow the Lord because He knew what was good for him.

Soon the train entered the fishing village of Hull. Hudson grabbed his suitcase and walked onto the platform. Once he was outside the train station, he took the paper out of his pocket and looked carefully for Charlotte Street. It was a walk of about fifteen minutes. Full of courage he started off.

It was not long before he reached the wealthy neighborhood of Hull. According to the paper he was still going in the right direction. He should reach his destination after two more streets. Indeed, he soon found the doctor's practice of Robert Hardey. The directions had been correct. The house at number 3 was covered in ivy.

Hudson straightened out his coat, checked his hat and dropped the knocker on the door of the attractive house. The door was opened immediately. A tall man appeared in the doorway. He welcomed Hudson warmly. "Welcome, Hudson Taylor. We were expecting you. Pleased to meet you. I am Doctor Hardey. Come on in, my boy."

* * *

A few months later, Father Hudson opened the latest of the many letters that Hudson had sent. Feeling somewhat proud, he put it down on the table. Hudson had learned a lot since he had started living with Doctor Hardey. He did all the bookkeeping, handed out medicine, took care of wounds and assisted with childbirths. In addition to that, he was taking courses at the medical college. All those things were a good preparation for later on.

It was a pity that he could not stay in Doctor Hardey's house any longer. But the doctor had made him a good offer. He would pay the rent if Hudson would live with his Aunt Hannah. And he was sure that she would take good care of him. Hannah and her husband Richard were not rich but they were very generous. Father was convinced that they would treat Hudson as if he were their own child.

* * *

Tired after a long day of work, Hudson entered his small one-room apartment. It was cold and dark. Sometimes he missed Aunt Hannah's good care, but he did not regret the decision he had made last fall to find a cheaper place to live. He did not want to be an "easy"

Christian. The way he now lived allowed him to give a tenth of his salary to the Lord and that made him happy.

As soon as the fireplace was burning and the oil lamp spread a soft, golden light, Hudson looked around in satisfaction. He was very happy with this simple, working-class cottage on the riverside. Captain Finch was hardly ever home and his wife was a sweet Christian. He only had to pay three shillings a week as rent. He had noticed that the area was quite poor. The sandy road leading to the house was a big mud pool when it rained. At night he could not see anything because there was no lighting. But everything had worked out well, despite his mother's worries that he would end up in the ditch one day.

There were also many good things here, especially now that spring was on its way. During the winter he had seen several kingfishers. Beautiful! The day before he had seen that the waterhens had cautiously started to build their nests among the reeds. He also felt at home in the church he attended and he had found several friends. Some friends firmly believed that it would not be long before he would go to China. That is why he had made the resolution to live even more frugally. During the last few weeks he had eaten honey cake and herring for breakfast, and in the evening eaten peas instead of potatoes. He didn't mind; he had not been hungry at all yet. He enjoyed eating cheap food. Who knew what type of food he would have to eat in China and how much money he would have to live off.

He thought of his father and mother. He decided to write Mother the letter which he had promised her. Mother was a faithful writer.

Drainside, March 22, 1852

Dear Mother,
Things are going well here. Don't worry about the way I live. I feel healthy. I just bought red cabbage for a penny and I preserved it with vinegar which cost three pennies and a half. It filled a whole pot.

In the meantime I have also discovered a store where cheese is even cheaper. By living this way, I can give 60% of my income to poor people in this area. There is a lot of poverty among young families and older people here. And what is even more important, I feel that the Lord approves of the way I live. Every day it is a joy for me to live for Him and with Him. I want to do nothing else. This way of life is also a good preparation for my life in China. I want to do my best to trust in the Lord even more unconditionally. I no longer want to be dependent on what others give me, but I want to expect all things from Him. In China I will also not have anyone to fall back on.

I should stop now, Mother.
Greet Father, Amelia and Louisa also.

Your son,
Hudson Taylor

7. Trusting in God Alone

1852

"Oh sir, can you please come along with me? I don't know what to do! My wife is going to die!"

Frightened, Hudson Taylor looked at the man who was suddenly standing beside him.

It was ten o'clock on Sunday evening. He was on his way home. This evening he had visited several poor families, like he always did on Sunday evenings.

By the light of the moon Hudson could just barely see the man's face. He did not know him. The man spoke with a strong Irish accent. Hudson knew that he was taking a risk by walking in this district of Hull in the evening. There was a lot of violence and crime. Even the police did not dare to walk the streets.

"You are Doctor Hardey's assistant and you told us about God not too long ago, didn't you?" the man panted.

"Indeed," Hudson said as he tried to keep his composure.

"Come along quickly and pray for us. I have no money for the priest. I have to pay eighteen cents for him to pray for my wife. We are almost starving to death."

"Why didn't you ask for help at the city hall if you don't have any money?" Hudson asked in surprise.

"I did. I can get it tomorrow but that does not help me today. Come, please go along with me!" He pulled Hudson's coat violently.

Hudson followed the man through the narrow alleys. What should he do? He could not really give the man his own money, could he? He had only one coin left, a half crown. That was all he had. This week Doctor Hardey had again forgotten to pay him his salary for the past three months but Hudson had firmly resolved not to ask for it. He wanted to rely on God alone. During the last two days he had constantly prayed that God would help him. For just a moment the thought flashed through his mind that if he had two shillings and a six-pence, he would be able to give the man a shilling. The thought startled him. He also felt that the deep peace, which had been in his heart during the evening when he had spoken about the service of God, had suddenly disappeared.

In the meantime they had arrived at the square where some angry residents had ripped to pieces the tracts which he had distributed there a few weeks ago. They had even threatened him with the words, "Don't ever come back, because you won't leave our district alive!"

"Lord, help me!" Hudson begged softly. "Protect me and give me wisdom."

"I live in this street," the man pointed. "We're taking these stairs."

Carefully the two men climbed the dirty, rickety staircase. They were met by the sound of crying children.

As they stepped into the upper apartment room, Hudson saw five skinny children with frightened eyes and an exhausted mother with a newborn baby. They were living in horrible conditions.

"Don't worry, children," he said in a soothing voice. "Don't cry. God is a loving Father in heaven. He can take care of you and also of your father and mother."

Immediately it was as if someone said to him, "You hypocrite! You can say that God is love but you don't even want to give away half a crown!"

The thought confused Hudson for a minute but he did not want to give in to it. He proposed to say a prayer. He knelt down by the mother's bed and begged, "Our Father, which art in heaven … Wilt Thou please take pity on this poor woman and her family! Thou knowest how hungry they are." But as he said these words, it was as if someone gripped his throat. He was indeed praying, but … did he believe in the Heavenly Father? And was he prepared to give everything that he possessed to these people?

He ended his prayer much sooner than he had intended to and stood up.

Again the man took him by the arm and begged, "Sir, if you can help us, please help us for God's sake!"

Then Hudson could no longer resist. It was as if the money in his pocket was on fire.

"Here," he said to the man, "here is everything I have. I believe that God will take care of you and of me. You may have my very last money."

At first the man was speechless. But when Hudson put the money into his hand, his eyes began to sparkle.

"Thank you, thank you," he stammered.

As Hudson walked through the deserted streets of Hull a short while later, his heart rejoiced. It was a pitch dark night, but it was light again in his heart. He was filled with peace. He firmly believed that God would take care of him!

* * *

The next morning Hudson heard a noise outside as he was eating breakfast. He looked out the window. It sounded as if someone was knocking on the front door. Was it the mailman? So early on Monday morning? He put his spoon down and listened. It was the mailman! Well, it must not be for him. He picked up his spoon again and took a big spoonful of oatmeal. Perhaps a message from the captain? After the front door was closed he immediately heard a knock on his door.

"Good morning, Hudson," Mrs. Finch smiled. "That is out of the ordinary. The mailman just dropped off an envelope for you."

"An envelope for me?"

Surprised, Hudson accepted the envelope. Who could have sent it? He did not recognize the handwriting. He tried to decipher the mail stamp but he could not read it. Mrs. Finch's wet hands had made it illegible. Carefully he felt the envelope. It was not only a letter; the envelope was too thick for that.

Full of curiosity, he opened it. He saw a small package with a white sheet of paper wrapped around it. Carefully he unwrapped the paper. He could not understand it at all. There were two velvet children's gloves. Why had someone sent them to him?

As he held the children's gloves in front of him, something fell out and dropped to the floor. He heard a tinkling sound.

Dumbfounded, Hudson stared at the floor. What? It was … a golden coin!

He quickly shoved his chair back and picked up the coin. It was a half pound coin! It was more than four times the value of what he had given to the sick woman's husband the night before!

"Bless the Lord, O my soul!" he exclaimed in delight. "Oh, how can I ever thank Him enough!"

He was rendered speechless. His trust in God had not been put to shame.

8. Money Worries Again

1852

"This has been quite a week, Hudson," Doctor Hardey sighed, as he sat down in one of the easy chairs in his doctor's office.

"That's true, Doctor Hardey," Hudson answered absentmindedly. He looked at the plumes of steam which slowly coiled up out of the cast iron pan on the stove.

Hudson slowly stirred the water to see if the medicine was hot enough. He felt hot, and not only because of the rising steam. He had to control himself from heaving a deep sigh every now and then. He was very worried. But if Doctor Hardey heard him sigh, he would certainly ask what was wrong. And Hudson would rather bite off his tongue than honestly tell the doctor that he was in great need. Doctor Hardey still had not paid him his salary and that was causing problems. Tonight he would have to pay his rent to Mrs. Finch. She also needed the money badly. During the past two weeks, he had used the golden coin from the children's glove to buy food, but that money was now gone. All through the day he had prayed, "Lord, wilt Thou please remind Doctor Hardey that he has still not paid my salary? I want to rely on Thee alone."

But still nothing had happened.

Doctor Hardey was pleased with his hard-working assistant. It was almost five o'clock. He was happy that he had managed to finish all his visits before Sunday and that all the prescriptions had been written out.

As he stirred the pan, the thought crossed Hudson's mind: "This is the right moment! Can you not ask for your salary because Mrs. Finch needs the money? You're not asking for it for yourself!" But as soon as the thought arose, he quickly suppressed it. He did not want to do that!

"Did you hear what I said, Hudson?" the doctor asked in a friendly tone of voice.

Hudson felt even warmer yet.

"Excuse me, Doctor Hardey. I was thinking of something else."

"That's okay, my boy," Doctor Hardey continued. "I said that it is a privilege that we always have a short preparation for the Sabbath together on Saturday afternoon. Do you know what portion of the Bible you want to speak about tomorrow in the working class district?"

"No, not quite. I want to spend some more time tonight preparing myself."

"So you're not planning to go home anytime soon?"

"No, there is still enough work to …"

Suddenly Doctor Hardey jumped up out of his chair. Hudson was startled. What was going on?

"Say Hudson," the doctor remarked, "Do you know what I'm wondering? Did I actually pay you your salary for the last three months?"

Hudson's throat felt as if it closed suddenly! He had to swallow a few times before he could give an answer. His employer's question moved him deeply. Was the Lord not showing clearly that He would take care of him?

He quickly turned around again and checked the pan, worried that Doctor Hardey would see his emotion. He tried to make his voice sound as normal as possible. "No, you haven't paid me yet."

"Oh, I'm so sorry that I forgot," Doctor Hardey said sincerely. "Didn't I tell you when you had just come that you had to ask me for your salary if I forgot? Oh, how could I have been so dumb! And I brought the money I received from my patients this week to the bank this afternoon. Otherwise I could have paid you right away."

For a minute Hudson felt everything moving around him. A nauseous feeling cut off his breath. How could this be? He thought God would help him and now this …

"The medicines are done, Doctor Hardey," he said as he took the pan off the stove and brought it to the adjacent room.

"Excellent, Hudson. Don't work too late tonight. I'm going home. See you in church tomorrow!"

"Good. See you tomorrow."

* * *

That evening Hudson felt at ease as he closed the Bible. The Bible study had given him new strength and courage. He was also happy that he had been able to finish the lectures for the next day. It was time for him to go home. It had become later than he intended. He figured that Mrs. Finch would be in bed by the time he arrived home. Normally he did not like that idea but today he was pleased with it because he was not able to pay her. Maybe there would be a solution for his problem on Monday. He was happy that he had the key to the back door which she had given him recently.

It was remarkable that, although he still did not have the money, he did not feel downcast like he had that afternoon. He did not know how his problem would be solved, but he could not believe that the Lord would disappoint him.

Hudson put on his coat, picked up his briefcase with one hand and was about to turn off the gaslight with the other when he heard someone in the garden. That had to be the doctor. His house was right beside the office. In surprise Hudson looked at the door where Doctor Hardey's laughing face had just appeared.

"You'll never guess what happened, Hudson!" the doctor chuckled. "I saw that you were still in the waiting room so I decided to come and tell you. Listen. One of my richest patients just stopped by to pay his bills. And that on Saturday evening! The man did not want to rest until he had paid everything. How can a person be like that? Could you write it in the ledger book right away? Can you imagine if I would forget that?"

Hudson walked straight to the mahogany cupboard where the doctor kept his accounts. He carefully filled in the amounts in the long columns.

As he put the ledger book away, the doctor suddenly said, "Say, Hudson, why don't I give you these bills? Just give me the change next week. I won't worry about it." And he handed Hudson a large bundle of bills.

"Thank you very much, Doctor Hardey," Hudson said politely. "It's nice that we can settle it this way." He could hardly contain himself. If only the doctor knew! He was not thinking in the first place about the money, but he was so happy that his trust in God had not been put to shame.

As he reached the outskirts of Hull, he held on to his briefcase even more tightly. There were a lot of shady characters walking around. But his heart rejoiced. He felt like shouting loudly, "I thank Thee, Lord. Thou doest what Thou hast promised. Therefore I dare to go to China, but only with Thee!"

He felt that a very important step had been made today with respect to his future. From now on he wanted to live even more out of faith. God was faithful and cared for him at His time.

9. The Hospital in London

1852

"We're dropping the anchor! It is not responsible for us to continue ..."

That was the message that was passed on from one passenger to another on a dark Saturday evening in September. The steamship had left Hull on Friday afternoon and was on its way to London.

Disappointed, Hudson walked back to his cabin. It was a pity but nothing could be done about it. God must have a reason for it. He would have liked to go on shore in this evening but God reigned. The thick fog surrounding the ship seemed to swallow up the pale light of the oil lamps which were supposed to illuminate the deck. It seemed as if the whole world were closed off. It was understandable that the captain had decided to drop the ship's anchor on the river Thames just before their final destination.

When he reached his cabin, Hudson took a map of China out of his suitcase and spread it out on the little table. How long would it be before he could start his journey to China? Sometimes he had the feeling that he could hardly wait. And yet ... time seemed to fly. The sixteen months he had spent with Doctor Hardey had flown by. He was thankful for everything that he had learned there and he would certainly benefit from it once he was a missionary in China. But he wanted to specialize even further in medicine. His medical basis was still too narrow, especially if he wanted to work on a medical mission post. His thoughts drifted back to four months ago. He had been excited when he had read in the May edition of *The Harvester* that the Chinese Evangelization Society (CES) wanted to send missionaries to China to open up a medical mission post there. He had immediately contacted the organization. They still remembered him from when he had spoken to them almost three years ago, shortly after his conversion. They had certainly not forgotten his longing to go to China. They could only accept one medical student and they had accepted him! After his studies at the hospital in London, he would be sent out to China. The board of CES had even offered to pay for all his costs. Unbelievable! It could only be the Lord's hand.

He had thought about the wonderful offer for a few days. He had fervently prayed that he might know the will of God. Was he allowed to accept the money or not? It seemed like some sort of trial because at the same time his father had offered to pay for his studies. Yet, Hudson knew what God asked of him. He would not accept money from anyone. The Lord had pointed him to the words, "Be still and know that I am God."

He remembered the letter he had written to his mother on August 27, a few weeks ago. He still believed what he had written then: He wanted to surrender himself to the Lord. And never before had he felt so much peace in his heart.

That's why he had not been worried whether there would be an opening for him to study in the hospital in London. He also did not want to rely on Uncle Benjamin who lived there and was friends with several doctors. God would fight for him.

He decided to read Psalm 37 once more as a preparation for the Sabbath and for this new time in London.

* * *

Six weeks later a happy Hudson was walking through the big city of London. He was on his way to the hospital. Every day it took him at least two hours to walk there from the house where he was living. He did not want to take the bus because he felt that six pennies a day was too expensive. He could not afford that. He told himself that walking every day would be good for his physical condition.

Behind him Hudson heard the loud, cutting sound of the rattling wheels of a carriage which was getting very close to him. Startled, he jumped to the side of the road and continued on his way.

What would he be doing today? Imagine if he had to assist with a surgery just like he had done the day before. Oh, how the man had screamed! Understandable, since the only anaesthesia he had received was alcohol. Hudson had felt uncomfortable as he and a few other

nurses had tried to restrain the poor man. But apparently that was the usual method in the hospital. The nurses were not too concerned about it. And the doctor had said matter-of-factly, "I like to hear the patient yelling. That's a sign he is still alive! You'll get used to it, Hudson."

Time would tell. But he certainly would never get used to the bad language his fellow students used occasionally. Sometimes the things they dared to say frightened him.

Living in the big city of London was totally different from living in Mrs. Finch's quiet house on the shores of Drainside. There he could enjoy the birds and nature. Here he walked every day among screaming merchant men who loudly offered their wares on the street.

But he also saw beautiful things every day. For instance, the imposing building of St. Paul's Cathedral. What a beautiful church that was!

Yes, he had many reasons to be thankful. It had only taken four weeks before the hospital had given him permission to begin his medical studies. He had also soon found a place to live. Surprisingly enough, it was close to where his mother's brother lived. His cousin Tom, who lived around the corner with Uncle Benjamin, had offered to share a room with him. That would save him a lot of money.

He tried to live as cheaply as possible. On his way home tonight he was going to stop by the bakery. This baker sold a whole loaf of bread for only two pennies and it tasted very good. He was going to ask if they could cut the loaf in half so he could eat it in one day: one half in the morning and the other half in the evening. For lunch he bought apples. That way he only spent three pennies a day on food, which was even cheaper than when he was staying with Mrs. Finch.

Thinking back to his scanty meals in Drainside, he suddenly remembered what he had promised Captain Finch a few months ago. He had almost forgotten! He should not forget to visit the shipping office soon. Every month he faithfully picked up a part of the captain's salary there and sent it on to Mrs. Finch. Unfortunately he did not have time to pick up the money this week. He was busy with a very important investigation which would determine his scholarship. That's why he had decided the evening before that he would send part of his own money to Mrs. Finch. As soon as he had more time, he would go to the shipping office to ask for the captain's salary for himself. In the end, it would make no difference.

Soon Hudson arrived at the gate of the hospital.

10. In Danger of Life

1852

Dumbfounded, Hudson stared at the shipping office clerk behind the counter. How could that be true? He just could not believe it!

He had just asked for half of the monthly salary of Captain Finch. But the clerk had told him that the captain no longer worked for the company. He had become a gold digger and had disappeared without a trace.

Hudson reeled from the news. "But ... sir, do you understand that I cannot do without the money?" he stammered.

"I certainly understand," the man answered, "but I have to obey the company's regulations. I cannot just give you the money."

It dawned on Hudson that he had lost his money. And he did not want to ask for it from his former landlady. The woman had no money to pay him back.

Disappointed, Hudson said goodbye to the man and left the building. He walked back home, his hands deep in his coat pockets. That was a big disappointment!

Suddenly, it was as if he heard someone say, "Be careful for nothing." It startled him. Was he allowed to be of little faith? Had the Lord not promised to take care of him? He became angry with himself. He had to stop feeling sad and trust in God alone. The Lord would give deliverance at His time. He had done that all along and He would also do it in this situation!

* * *

The next morning it was very quiet in the surgery room of the London hospital. The students were concentrating intently on dissecting a body. The deceased had died from an unknown virus, so dissecting the body would be instructive and important, but ... also not without risk. The surgeon who trained the students had given them a special warning to be very cautious. A person could receive a deadly infection from doing this work.

Although Hudson was not feeling very well, he did his best to hide it from the others. If he could not continue at all, then he would go home earlier. He felt stressed because it seemed as if his condition was worsening. Strange actually. On his way to the hospital this morning he had felt fine. Now he occasionally felt as if he were sweating. He decided to go for a drink of water. Good! It gave him some relief. He was happy when the assignment was over.

That afternoon, during a lecture about the operation, he felt more and more miserable. He could hardly write anymore. His right arm was hurting terribly.

As he was picking up his belongings, he asked one of the doctors, "Doctor, do you know what's wrong with me? I feel very miserable and I have a lot of pain in my right arm."

The doctor looked at him searchingly. "Tell me exactly how you feel," he said sternly.

As Hudson described his condition, the doctor looked more and more concerned.

"Do you know what I'm afraid of?" he said anxiously. "That you cut yourself during the dissection this morning. Show me your hands."

Bewildered, Hudson held out his hands. Carefully, he and the doctor looked at them from all sides, but neither was able to find any cuts.

Suddenly he remembered what had happened the night before. While putting a few sheets of paper together he had cut himself with the sharp point of a metal wire.

As he related this, the surgeon looked visibly frightened.

"My boy," he said worriedly, "this will be your end. Go home as soon as possible and settle what needs to be settled. Your time is short!"

For a moment Hudson was filled with panic. What? He? Would he die now? Then he could not go to China and had God not promised that?

Suddenly his panic left him and a feeling of peace came over him.

He looked at the doctor and said, "Doctor, that is not possible. I have to go to China. God has called me to go there."

The doctor shook his head sadly. "Believe me, my boy. You are in a serious condition. You don't have much time to lose. You will become more and more ill. Rent a carriage and go home as quickly as you can."

Hudson straightened his back and answered politely, "And even if I am mistaken, I may know that after my death I will go to my Master. I am going home now because you want me to but I am leaving without fear. The Lord takes care of me."

* * *

Hudson was lying in bed with his eyes closed. It had already been a few weeks since he had left the hospital after he had contracted an infection. It was truly a miracle that he was still alive! Two fellow students who had also been infected had died in the meantime, but he was still alive.

He could still remember clearly what had happened that day. When he had arrived at home, he had asked the maid for hot water and then he had cut his finger open to get rid of the infected blood. He did not remember much of what had happened from then on, only that he had fainted. He did remember that he was lying in bed when he revived. Uncle Benjamin was there, along with a friend who was a doctor. At first the man did not want to do anything for him because it would be of no use. It would only cost money. But Uncle Benjamin would have none of that. He immediately offered to pay all the bills for his nephew.

Hudson smiled when he thought of the past weeks. He had never eaten such lavish meals. Uncle Benjamin had not spared any cost; nothing was too expensive. He had bought everything that was healthy and what the doctor prescribed. Even pork chops.

He was thankful that he had recovered enough so that he could go for a short walk close to home now and then. Today he wanted to try and go as far as the park.

He carefully got out of bed, looked for his coat and walked down the long stairway.

It was quite an effort for him. He was glad that there was a bench downstairs. He had just sat down when the front door opened.

"Hey Hudson!" a voice said in surprise. "How is that possible? How did you get downstairs?"

The doctor walked towards him with a surprised look on his face.

"I went down by myself, doctor" Hudson said modestly. "I practise every day so I can walk a bit farther each time."

The doctor looked at him from head to toe. As he rubbed his beard with one hand, he said softly, "Hudson, do you know what would be good for you? If you would go to the countryside for awhile. It would improve your health. If you start working too soon you may never fully regain your strength."

At first the thought startled Hudson. He? To Barnsley? That was impossible!

Father and Mother did not even know that he was sick. They were under the impression that he was busy with his tests and exams. He had made Uncle Benjamin and his cousin Tom promise him that they would not say anything to his parents. He had done that because he wanted to see whether he was able to rely on God alone, even when sick or in need of money.

"I'll think about it, Doctor," Hudson said softly. "Thank you for your advice."

Suddenly Hudson felt tired again. He felt a very strong inner conflict. If he would go to his parents, his money worries would be over. Father would certainly help him out. But that was exactly what he did not want. He also did not have the money to travel home.

"Dear Father in heaven," he whispered. "Wilt Thou help me? Thou knowest what I need. Wilt Thou take care of me?"

11. Exciting Developments in China

1852-1853

The shrill, high tones of the front doorbell sounded through the reception area of the shipping company. The clerk quickly stamped a letter, pushed his chair back and walked towards the counter. "What can I do for you?" he asked casually. He startled as he took a closer look at the visitor. The man looked very pale and skinny! For a second he thought, Where have I met this boy? But he could not recall exactly where.

"Good afternoon, sir," the guest answered. "I am Hudson Taylor and I am here again …"

It was quiet for a minute. The pale man gasped for breath.

"Please sit down," the clerk motioned. "There are enough chairs over here."

Hudson looked at the man gratefully. This was the same man who had told him earlier that Captain Finch had left for the gold mines.

As soon as Hudson caught his breath, the clerk asked him, "Are you feeling okay? You look very pale."

"I'm doing very well. I have been ill but I am recovering from my illness. The doctor advised me to go to the countryside to regain my health. I thought that before leaving London I should ask if you have possibly heard anything from Captain Finch."

"Oh, so that's you! I thought I recognized you from somewhere."

The man's eyes began to sparkle. "This is quite something. I'm glad you came so I can clear up a misunderstanding. The captain you are referring to still works for our company. Another employee with the same name has become a gold digger. So I can safely give you the money. I know it will be in good hands."

Hudson could hardly believe his ears. So … there was nothing wrong with Captain Finch … and he would receive his money.

Before he had a chance to say anything, the man behind the counter asked, "It's lunch time. Would you mind joining me for lunch?"

* * *

Hudson was very happy when he got on the horse trolley a short time later. He now had enough money to pay for the trip home. The Lord had taken care of that in a miraculous way.

He also wanted to visit Uncle Benjamin's doctor. The man had refused payment for all the visits, medicines and advice. But Hudson wanted to tell him that he had received money from the Lord to pay for all the bills.

When he met the doctor and offered to pay for everything, the man refused. He said, "No Hudson, that's not going to happen. You are still studying. I do not want to accept any money from you."

Deep in his heart Hudson pitied the man. He was a famous doctor but he lived without the Lord. He was just as poor as the people in China who lived without God.

Suddenly Hudson could no longer be silent.

"Doctor," he said, deeply moved, "it is partly thanks to you that I'm sitting here. The Lord has taken care of me. It is the wish of my heart that you may learn to know the faith in the same God, because only then can you be truly rich and happy. As you know, I am studying medicine because I would like to go to China to tell the people there about God. When I left Hull and came to London, I resolved that I would not accept money from anyone. That's why I rejected the payment from my father and from the mission organization CES. They wanted to pay for my entire education. But I did not want to accept the money. I believe in a God who takes care of me, in a God who works miracles. And whether you believe it or not, God helped me when I prayed yesterday as I walked from my house to the shipping office."

The doctor put his hand in front of his mouth. "But that's impossible, Hudson!" he cried out. "Did you walk three kilometres?"

"Yes, Doctor," Hudson insisted, "it is true. And the same God who gave me the strength to do that has taken care that I received money today, exactly enough to pay for the trip to my parents."

The doctor stared at him in utter amazement. He simply could not understand it.

"I would give everything to serve that God," he said softly.

* * *

It was Saturday, June 4, 1853. At the CES office in London, Mr. Charles Bird, the secretary of the mission organization for China, had just signed a letter which he had written. The board of CES wanted to have the letter delivered to Hudson Taylor, the young medical student, as soon as possible. They believed that now was the best time to send missionaries to China.

Because of the Taiping Rebellion, which had broken out in China in the spring of 1852 and which was still continuing at the time, many Christians believed that China was ripe for the Gospel. The government of Taiping, a Chinese population group, was introducing different reforms. They wanted to break permanently with the Chinese tradition. They removed the requirement that civil servants write exams about the knowledge of old Chinese wisdom. Instead, they wanted to test their knowledge of the Bible! They wanted men and women to be equal. Women's feet were no longer allowed to be bound to keep them small. There was a ban on opium, gambling, tobacco, alcohol and slavery. Having more than one wife was no longer permitted. In short, the entire Chinese society was changing. And the insurgents kept advancing. In March they had captured Nanjing, the former capital of China. This gave them power over the Great Canal which was the main waterway between the north and south.

It would not be long before they would control Beijing. And when that had been accomplished, the Gospel could be brought to China. It was hard to believe.

Mr. Bird shook his head as he closed the envelope. Just as he put the envelope in the mail folder he heard a knock on the door. "Come in," he said absentmindedly.

"Good afternoon, Mr. Bird," Hudson Taylor said cheerfully as he closed the door behind him.

"Hudson Taylor …"

In utter amazement Mr. Bird stared at him. "How is it possible? I just wrote you a letter on behalf of our board with the question if you can go to China on short notice. And you're here before I can mail the letter."

Surprised, Hudson Taylor sat down. "This must be the Lord's doings," he said. "It cannot be otherwise. Since the time that I read in the magazine *The Harvester* about the developments in China, the temptation to end my study in medicine has definitely increased. Doctor Brown, the surgeon with whom I am presently studying, has earnestly advised me to continue my studies for one more year. Then I can complete my exams for the College of Physicians. But I cannot continue. How many people in China would I be able to reach with God's Word in one year? I no longer want to spend my time finishing my studies. My heart is in China."

12. The Voyage

1853

With a loving gesture Mother Taylor straightened the bed in Hudson's cabin. Finally the moment of departure had arrived. Today, Monday morning, September 19, 1853, Hudson would leave for China. Maybe it would be the very last time that she could make his bed. In a short time all the baggage would be on board the ship and the cables would be loosened. The moment of farewell was coming very close.

Tears welled up in her eyes as she looked around. If everything went well, her son would spend the next five months in this cabin before he arrived in China. The captain had been nice enough to have the walls painted in nice, bright colours, especially for Hudson. Besides the crew, there was only a Chinese boy named Fang aboard. But no matter how nice the cabin looked, it did not lessen the distance between her and her son!

She felt a lump in her throat. Would she ever see Hudson again? Oh, what a difficult moment!

Was she then not willing to give up her child for the Lord and His service? She certainly was, but she loved him very much.

It was also difficult for her husband. She remembered his tear-stained eyes as the train began to move at the Liverpool station. It was too bad that he had been required to go home earlier, but the pharmacy could not remain closed. Hudson had run alongside the train as long as he could. Saying goodbye to his father had been very difficult for him.

For the last time Mother Hudson looked around the cabin. Well, she should go upstairs. The ship's horn had sounded already. She wiped her eyes and straightened up. She should control her emotions, also for Hudson. He was very brave. Last night at the hotel he had read John 14: "Let not your heart be troubled: ye believe in God, believe also in Me. In My Father's house are many mansions." The words had greatly encouraged her. It was better for her to count her blessings than to be so sad. Had she not always prayed that God would use Hudson in His service?

They had just sung the beautiful hymn by John Newton, together with Hudson's friend Arthur Taylor and Rev. Plunkett, here in the cabin:

> *How sweet the Name of Jesus sounds*
> *in a believer's ear!*
> *It soothes our sorrows, heals our wounds,*
> *and drives away our fear.*

She wanted to hold on to that. They had earnestly prayed together. She did not doubt that Hudson was following God's way. And yet ... tears welled up in her eyes again. It was so difficult ...

* * *

A few hours later Hudson Taylor looked around in surprise. He could hardly believe his eyes. Where was he? What was the thing that was swinging from the ceiling? It looked as if the floor was moving. He got up and suddenly he remembered. He was on his way to China! He was lying in his cabin on the *Dumfries*. The lamp that was hanging from the ceiling was swinging back and forth. He wondered whether the medicine was making him dizzy. The farewell had also been difficult. Arthur Taylor, his friend who would leave in two weeks as a missionary, and the old Rev. Plunkett had left first. Then his mother had left the ship, but as soon as she had reached the dock, her legs had begun to shake. Poor mother. He had lost control. He had run to her and had put his arms around her. "Dear Mother," he had said, "we are not saying farewell forever. Once we will see each other again. You know which important task I am leaving you for, right? To tell the Chinese people about the Lord Jesus. They have never heard of him!"

He had quickly jumped back on board and run to his cabin. There he had quickly written on the first page of his Bible, *The love of Christ passeth all knowledge*. Then he had thrown the Bible to his mother.

As the ship left the dock he had waved to her with his handkerchief as long as he possibly could. After she had disappeared from view, he had fastened his belongings and taken a sleeping pill. The farewell had touched him deeply.

Hudson struggled to remain standing upright. It seemed as if he was overcome with sleep! Suddenly he understood. He was not dizzy but the ship was swaying back and forth quite a bit. He moved the curtain aside and became frightened when he saw how high the waves were splashing. The white crests were being flung against the window of his cabin.

As soon as he arrived on deck, one of the sailors shouted, "Be careful! We're on the Irish Sea. We're in the middle of a western storm. It will be a few days before the weather becomes calmer! You'd better go downstairs!"

* * *

A few days later great panic broke out on board the *Dumfries*. "Look, there's the lighthouse!" the helmsman pointed. He could hardly make himself understood because of the raging wind which roared around them.

"We're in danger of our lives. We're heading straight for the coast!" The ship heaved from left to right, from right to left. The waves towered high above the ship which was adrift.

"I have never experienced such a wild sea!" Captain Morris shouted back. "If God does not help us, we are totally lost. Especially because night is falling …" His voice was lost in a terrible cracking which could suddenly be heard above the roaring of the foaming sea.

"Help! Grab the mast. We're losing it!"

One of the side beams of the big mast had been split in half by the tremendous power of the storm!

"Another problem! Quick, tie up the rope!" the captain called out in a stern voice.

Two sailors struggled against the wind towards the thick coil of rope in the middle of the ship. They had to grab hold of different things. They were in grave danger of being dragged over the deck into the surging sea by the raging waves.

As soon as they grabbed hold of the coil, they dragged the heavy rope along to the side beam and tried to fasten it.

At that moment it was not only storming at sea but also in Hudson's heart. He looked out the window with big eyes. They had bobbed on the raging sea for days already. Tonight they were about fifteen kilometres from the coast of Wales, according to the boatswain. To Hudson it felt as if they were moving closer and closer. He did not know what to do anymore.

"Lord," he begged, "Thou hast promised, 'Call upon Me in the day of trouble: and I will deliver thee, and thou shalt glorify Me.' Wilt Thou help us, Lord? Otherwise we will certainly be lost!"

He had heard the boatswain say that the life rafts would not be able to hold them in this weather. And they no longer had time to build a raft from masts and beams. The next half hour would be critical … The sailors literally did everything they could to steer the ship away from the coast.

Suddenly he felt more peaceful. Why was his faith so weak? After all, did he not know that God had sent him to China? Would God, who commanded the winds, not be able to calm the water about the ship? Oh, he firmly believed He could. And … if God's will was different, then He would certainly approve that Hudson had begun his journey.

Hudson heard screaming and shouting on the deck.

"Swing her around! We have to swing the ship around, sailors!"

But no matter what the sailors tried, nothing helped.

"Try to turn her the other way!" shouted the captain.

But no matter what they shouted, the ship was heading straight for the coast. The tall rocks were approaching at breakneck speed.

Hudson held his breath … He expected nothing else but that the ship would be smashed to pieces against the rocks which loomed in front of them.

Another eighty metres … only sixty metres …!

And then, suddenly … Oh, what was happening? How was it possible? The wind changed direction! The ship changed course and instead of being smashed against the rocks, it sailed past them at high speed.

It was a miracle from God …

The crew of the *Dumfries* looked around in mounting astonishment. How was this possible?

A short time later the storm was over. Only then it dawned on them: they were saved. The sky turned a soft red on the horizon. The night was past and a new day was dawning.

13. A Long Journey

1853-1854

December 31, 1853,

Dear Parents, Amelia, and Louisa,

It is a very different New Year's Eve for all of us. Sometimes I long very much to be with you for some time, but I know that's not possible. When I look back at the past year, I am amazed. How good God is! Until now everything has gone well. I mean it sincerely when I write: Ebenezer, hitherto hath the Lord helped us. Unto Him be all the glory.

A lot has happened since I said farewell to you on September 19. I wrote to you about the terrible storms we experienced. And about the times when there was no wind so we could not sail. I actually live in a very small world. On the one hand it is monotonous. We are always on board with the same 25 people. Every day we see the sea. But there are also a lot of things to do.

Sometimes I am unexpectedly called upon to serve as a doctor. Several times I have had to cut open an abscess. One time the captain had an abscess on his eyelid. And the cook had an abscess on his arm and another time on his hand. Sometimes I serve as a dentist. The other day I pulled out one of the boatswain's molars. And I have removed someone's tonsils.

But there is also time for recreation. I get along very well with the captain. Sometimes we work on algebra sums together. I am teaching him how to play the accordion. He is doing quite well already.

We have also gone swimming in the sea a few times but we have to watch out for sharks.

I often enjoy seeing the beautiful sunrises and sunsets. Oh, if only you could see that soft light, too!

Little Fang (you know he is the little Chinese boy) is teaching me how to pronounce the words from the Gospel of Luke which I wrote in a notebook together with my Cousin John.

During the day I sort out medicines and I put labels on the bottles. That will help me once I'm in China.

At Christmas we butchered one of the pigs that we had brought along. Occasionally we eat chicken or duck. The supply of meat is diminishing quite rapidly. But we are quite far already. If everything goes well, we will arrive in China by the end of February or the beginning of March.

At the beginning of December we rounded the Cape of Good Hope. In a few days we will reach the point where we are closest to Western Australia. From there we'll arrive at the route through the East Indian islands to the Pacific Ocean.

Sometimes it really touches me. On all these islands there are people who have never heard of God. Can you understand that there are so many men and women in England who live quietly in all luxury, while so many souls go lost? Are there not more people who want to sacrifice something for Him who gave His life to save the world? I don't understand it. This makes me sad.

Every Sunday we hold a church service on board, but alas ... I see so little fruit on my labour. Maybe the Lord wants to teach me in this way that I have to continue to sow His Word, even when I see no fruit. Together with the captain, the carpenter and the boatswain, we pray that God will work a change. They are also Christians. Our expectation is from the Lord. He is the Unchangeable who does what He promises.

Dear everyone, unfortunately I cannot mail this letter until we arrive in China. You will have to wait until then. We still have to sail about 5,000 kilometres before we arrive at our destination.

May God bless and keep you all!

Your son and brother,
Hudson Taylor

* * *

Hudson turned restlessly in his narrow bed. He felt as if he had heard something in his cabin. How was that possible? It was the middle of the night. What was going on? He hesitated for a minute, holding his breath. Yes, he could hear something. He heard someone sighing. He knew for sure!

Quickly he turned over.

The captain stared at him with frightened eyes. "Hudson, did I wake you up? Could you please come along to the deck with me?"

Surprised, Hudson got up, put his slippers on and quickly followed the captain who had already disappeared through the narrow walkway to the outside.

"Do you see those islands?" Captain Morris asked anxiously.

By the light of the moon Hudson stared at the dark spots in the distance.

"It is extremely dangerous to sail between those islands, Hudson. The map does not show exactly where they are."

"Let's pray, captain. God will take care of us," Hudson said softly. "He controls everything."

The two men knelt together in the soft moonlight. And the Lord heard their prayer! The next day the ship could sail for the Strait of Ombay without a problem.

Hudson's heart began to beat faster. He enjoyed seeing the woods and ravines which they passed. Sometimes he saw pastures. "How nice it will be to set foot on land!" he sighed.

* * *

On Sunday January 29, the captain, the carpenter, the boatswains and the sailors of the *Dumfries* were sitting around Hudson, just like they did every Sunday morning. The men listened intently to the message of God. Little Fang did too. He did not understand everything but he really enjoyed listening to the men singing while they were accompanied by Hudson Taylor on the accordion.

The captain stood up with an anxious expression on his face. He had already gone upstairs several times to check if the ship was still on course. He was worried. He walked to the deck with big steps. His hands gripped the railing tightly.

Yes, what he feared was true. There was still no wind at all. Because of the strong current in which they had ended up, they had sailed even farther off course. A short while ago they had been more than forty miles off course. Anxiety filled his heart. What should he do?

Land was approaching. The ship was being pushed along by the seemingly smooth sea. If they continued like this they would land on Papua New Guinea! Then the ship would either be smashed against the rocks or they would be attacked by the wild, painted savages!

"Hudson," the captain said nervously at the end of the service. "Something is wrong. We're heading in the wrong direction. It won't be long before we run aground on Papua New Guinea. I don't know what else we can do. I think we have done everything we could to get out of this dangerous current."

"Everything?" Hudson Taylor asked. "Have we really done everything, Captain?"

"Yes, I'm sure," the captain answered resolutely.

"I don't think so," Hudson countered. "We have forgotten the most important thing, Captain. We have not prayed yet. Don't we have four Christians on board here? Let each of us go to his own cabin and pray to God. The disciples were also astonished when Jesus ordered the sea to become calm. They said to each other, 'What manner of Man is this, that even the wind and the sea obey Him?' He is still the Same."

Immediately the captain called the carpenter and the boatswain and told them about Hudson's proposal. The men were in full agreement and went to their own cabins right away.

Hudson prayed fervently for the safety of the ship and its crew. But there was one thing that occupied his mind. "Lord," he begged, "the Chinese people have never heard of Thy wonderful Name. Help us, O God, and save us!"

He got up cheerfully after his prayer. All doubt had disappeared. He firmly believed that God had heard his prayer.

He quickly walked to the deck. "Go ahead and lower the corners of the main sail," he motioned to the first sailor.

The man looked at him with a haughty expression. "Who is the sailor here? You or I? Did you think that you know how to sail? It doesn't make any sense to lower the sail. There is not a breath of wind."

"The wind will pick up," Hudson insisted. "God in heaven will take care of us. Go ahead, lower the sail quickly. There is no time to lose. Otherwise the ship will be smashed against the rocks. Look! The sail is starting to billow up at the top …"

Surprised, the sailor looked up. Hudson was right.

"That's only a gust of wind," he muttered.

"Gust or no gust, the main sail has to come down!" Hudson said sternly.

The others on the deck watched in amazement.

"Hurry up!" the captain shouted. "Don't argue!"

Suddenly the ship changed course. It was heading in the right direction with billowing sails.

They were saved! It was not long before they left the rocks of Papua New Guinea behind them.

"If things go well it will be about one week before we reach Shanghai, Hudson!" the captain said gratefully.

14. Arrival in Shanghai

1854

It was night. A mysterious silence hung over the big city of Shanghai. Suddenly the air was filled with dull, ear-piercing booms which shook the sleeping city awake.

Hudson Taylor immediately sat up in bed. What did he hear? Where was he? Confused, he looked around. The window of his bedroom rattled. He broke out in a sweat. Oh, he heard the noise again. It sounded like cannon shots!

He held his breath while he moved the curtain aside a little bit and cautiously peeked outside. The city walls were lit up. He could clearly distinguish the silhouettes of the soldiers on guard. Again he heard a cannon shot. The house was shaking on its foundations. Hudson cringed; he hardly dared to move. Occasionally he saw a light flashing. Although it was still pitch-black outside, the situation seemed serious. He heaved a sigh of relief when the noises stopped after awhile. How quiet everything seemed after that terrible racket! Feeling tired, he laid his head back down on the tattered pillows. His thoughts went back to yesterday, March 1, 1854, the day when he had finally set foot on land in Shanghai.

* * *

Tears of thankfulness had streamed down his cheeks as he had stood among the Chinese people. He had not known where to look. The people looked very different. They were small, had yellow skin and pitch-black hair. Most of them wore their hair in a straight braid down their backs. The men as well as women wore blue shirts and pants. They wore wide, yellow straw hats on their heads. Coolies[1] bowed deeply before the travellers, put their hands together and asked something which Hudson could not understand. After some

---

[1] A coolie was a Chinese worker or slave.

time he realized that in that way they were begging to carry the baggage. Later, they left the dock with the baggage fastened to long bamboo poles which they carried on their shoulders.

For a minute he had felt disappointment. There was no one on the dock who was waiting for him. Actually, he had not really known what to do. Finally he had decided to walk to the British Consulate, which he recognized when he saw the British flag blowing in the distance. Once he had arrived there he found out that the post office had closed already. That was too bad because he would not be able to find out if there were letters from home for him or money from CES, the mission organization which had sent him to China.

But he was happy, however, that the people at the consulate could tell him where Doctor Medhurst, one of the most important missionaries from England, lived. But the missionary was not home. He had gone on a trip with his wife. So Hudson was unable to personally hand him the letters which he had received in England. But he had found a place to stay. Doctor William Lockhart, the man who had managed to establish a hospital in Shanghai, had been very friendly and offered to let him stay at his place for the time being. Yes, things had worked out remarkably well. With open eyes Hudson stared in the darkness. What Doctor Lockhart had told him last night had kept him from falling asleep. The situation in Shanghai was very discouraging at the moment. The city was under the control of the Taiping rebels who wanted to do away with the old Chinese traditions. The emperor had sent fifty thousand soldiers to attack the city. The two sides were continually at war with each other. Because of this situation, housing, food and fuel had become abnormally expensive. He had arrived in China at a very inconvenient time. But he had a place to stay and even though the house was right beside the war zone, his life was in God's hand.

Outside it was still quiet. Hudson folded his hands and closed his eyes. He softly prayed, "Lord, let me not expect everything from people. He that dwelleth in the secret place of the most High shall abide under the shadow of the Almighty."

* * *

Dear Parents and Sisters,

Time flies. I have been living in China for over half a year already. It has not always been easy. The threat of war still looms. Especially the first while here I often asked myself: Why am I actually here? I could hardly do anything. I first had to study the Chinese language and learn the Chinese customs before I could start to make contact with people. But I'm glad things are improving. I no longer live with Doctor Lockhart but since August 30, I have been renting a cheap, wooden house close to the northern gate of Shanghai. It is even closer to the battlefront but I don't have enough money to pay for a safer house.

Everything is terribly expensive here. Our mission organization CES is unable to pay me more. In the meantime I am earning some money thanks to the Royal College of Physicians in London. I started my study of medicine again and I am performing experiments for them. I have already done several small surgeries during evangelizing trips which I sometimes make with John Burdon, a minister whom I met in Shanghai. The wife of this good friend died from cholera recently.

As far as the house goes, it is on the water. Every night I bring the gangplank inside and I have a burning light close by in case of danger. And the life-jacket you gave me, Mother, is right beside my bed. If necessary, I can put it on and jump into the water.

The house has several rooms. I also have a cook and a water carrier who work for me, so the Chinese respect me more. I also have a Christian who is working for me. His name is Si. He helps me to translate my prayers and reads verses from the Bible to the servants and the people from the neighbourhood who attend our services. Si also teaches ten boys and five girls. In addition, a few people come to my medical clinic each day. Because of all these contacts, I am better able to make myself understood in Chinese. Twice a day I pray with all who live here. I can speak the Mandarin dialect quite well already.

But I have to be honest and confess that it is not always easy. I sometimes feel very lonely. Mother, if only you knew how often I read your letters!

Father, could you also write sometime? I would greatly appreciate that. It is not easy to be alone all the time but I don't want to complain. How much I still have when I think of the Lord Jesus, who had no stone on which to lay His head. He was much lonelier than I can ever feel. Will you please pray for me?

Your son and brother,
Hudson Taylor

15. The Gospel in the Interior Also

1855

"Sir, please sir, don't do it! It is such a dangerous plan! I'm sure you won't come back alive. Believe us, the city of Tongzhou is known as 'Satan's throne'. We know the population. They have murdered a lot of foreigners already."

With their hands folded, the two Chinese teachers looked imploringly at Hudson Taylor and John Burdon.

"We did not have any problems yesterday," Hudson remarked in surprise. "We even spread the Gospel in the interior among thousands of people who visited the temples of the idols. I would not be able to sleep one more night if we would not tell the people in Tongzhou that there is a God in heaven who is stronger than all their idols."

"That's true," John Burdon nodded. "You know what? We'll go by ourselves, Hudson. Both of you can go back to our two boats by the Yangtze River and wait for us."

Disappointed, the two Chinese men walked back to the river through the rain. The missionaries probably thought that they were too cowardly to go along, but that was not true. Their plan for today was far too dangerous!

As soon as the two teachers left, Hudson Taylor and John Burdon, together with their servant, picked up the luggage which they had put in bags and were on their way. They were carrying quite a few tracts and parts of the Bible to hand out among the people. "Just over a year ago I could not have imagined this," Hudson Taylor said after awhile. "I'm glad that I'm becoming more and more familiar with the language. It was a good plan to work not only in Shanghai but also to visit the interior together."

"That's true," Burdon nodded. "And ... in this way we can hit two birds with one stone. While I hand out tracts and parts of the Bible and proclaim the Gospel, you can help the sick. The only problem is that the weather is not very favourable today. It seems like the rain is starting to come down even harder. I'm afraid it will be evening before we reach the city if we have to trudge through the mud like this."

"Oh sir … look!" the servant exclaimed. "Look at that house over there. There are wheelbarrows and coolies for rent. Maybe that's a good idea!"

"Excellent!" Hudson Taylor said. "That's the perfect solution." Resolutely he walked towards the coolies and asked them if they could be brought to Tongzhou.

The coolies bowed deeply. They were very happy that they could earn some money. They drove the wheelbarrows out of the dilapidated shed as quickly as possible.

In the meantime their own servant walked back and forth nervously. "Um … sir …," he asked, searching for the right words. "Um, do you think that … I can … go back to the two Chinese teachers on the boat?"

Hudson Taylor and John Burdon looked at each other. They realized that their servant did not dare to go any further.

"Go ahead," Hudson nodded. "But we are continuing."

* * *

"Look over there!" Hudson pointed out into the distance.

A few men were standing by the city gate. It looked like they were busily discussing something. But as soon as they noticed the two strangers, they started shouting and calling out, "Hey guizi[1], what are you doing here?"

Frightened, Hudson and John saw the men running towards them at high speed.

"Get out of here! You are guizi!" they screamed.

Before John Burdon realized what was going on, he felt a terrible pain in his shoulder. A big, drunken man had hit him very hard.

For a minute Hudson's head was spinning. What was going on?

Then he straightened his back and said sternly, "Bring us to the head of the city!"

---
[1] Black devils

He hoped that by acting sternly he could impress the men.

"What do you think?" one of the bandits shouted. "Do you think we'll listen to you? You are a bunch of Taipei rebels. You're only coming here to make this area unsafe."

Threateningly, the big, violent man walked towards Hudson Taylor. "Be quiet, you!" he warned, his eyes flickering with rage. "I'll show you who is the boss around here!" Furiously, he hurled Hudson to the ground a few times. He hit him wherever he could. Then he grabbed the missionary by the throat with his big hands and shook him back and forth violently.

Hudson gasped for breath. He thought the man was going to kill him.

John Burdon saw the great danger his friend was in. He took a New Testament from his bag and called out, "Would you like to have this?"

But that made the men even angrier.

"What? How dare you! Do we have handcuffs?" the giant bellowed.

"Just drag them along to the city!" one of the men called.

"No. Let's just slaughter them right here!" another one shouted.

There was a brief moment of commotion while the cruel men argued with each other.

"Burdon," Hudson said with great effort, "think of the apostles. They rejoiced that they were worthy to suffer for the sake of Christ."

Burdon nodded at his friend thankfully.

Suddenly Hudson realized that he had his identity papers on him. As fast as he could he put his hand in his pocket and proudly held up the paper.

"Look what I have here. This paper is proof that we are no rebels!"

For a minute the men were dumbfounded. They had not expected that.

"And ... I demand that this paper be given to the highest official in your city," Hudson continued. "Bring us to him. Immediately."

The men grumbled for a short time but then they brought the two — albeit with great reluctance — to the city.

* * *

More and more people gathered in front of the house of the Chinese Mandarin who ruled over that part of the city. They wondered, "Who are these two foreigners? They look like they have been fighting. Why are they here?"

As a servant brought Hudson Taylor's identity papers to the Mandarin, John Burdon addressed the multitude which had flocked to the house. He told them about the Saviour, who was willing to leave heaven and come to this sinful world, to save poor sinners.

His hearers were surprised. They had never heard anything like that before.

Halfway during John's address, the Mandarin's servant returned. "It has been decided that your papers will be brought to an even higher Mandarin of Tongzhou. He will make a judgment. He lives in a different part of the city."

After hearing this, Hudson Taylor became angry. He did not like to be mocked with. "I don't accept this," he said indignantly. "Tell your Mandarin that we want to be carried there in litters. We have been so maltreated at the city gate that the journey would be too much for us."

The servant ran back to tell his master the proposal. A short while later, Burdon and Hudson were carried to the great Mandarin in the swinging litters.

* * *

Hudson Taylor and John Burdon were tired, but deeply thankful, when they arrived at the Yangtze River that evening and knocked on the window of their rented boat. They were safely home again.

The Chinese teachers and the servant were flabbergasted when they saw the two missionaries enter the boat.

"How is that possible? Did those cruel men in Tongzhou not kill you?" the servant stammered.

"As you see, the Lord has spared us," Hudson said. "For a moment we also thought that things were going wrong when we were attacked by a group of rough men by the city gate. We were first brought to one of the Mandarins. Later on we were brought to the room of Chen da Laoye. He is the highest authority in the city and he treated us very kindly. We told him who we were and with what purpose we had come. He wanted to have tea with us and offered us something to eat. We gave him and his officials New Testaments. Then we were allowed to visit the city and hand out our tracts to whomever we wanted."

The three who had stayed behind were speechless.

"And was there no one who maltreated you when you came outside the city?" the servant asked in disbelief.

"No one. From the moment that we left the city hall where the Mandarin lives, we had guards with us who protected us. They just brought us to the river. And so on our fifth journey we have also not been put to shame by Him who has called us to this task."

It was silent for a minute. Then the five men reverently knelt down to thank God who was so great and good!

16. A True Chinese

1855

Missionary Parker was sitting at his desk, his face red with anger as he quickly wrote. He could no longer tolerate it, so he had decided to write a letter. Since 1854, he had been living in Hudson Taylor's house in Shanghai, together with his wife and three children. For almost a year now he had seen with his own eyes that Hudson could hardly make ends meet with the money he received from the mission organization. If Doctor Medhurst had not offered his house to them, he and his family and Hudson Taylor would not even have had a place to stay. What was the board of the mission organization thinking? It was easy for them to make decisions in England. They should come here and have a look for themselves. They had not given one positive response to the many letters Hudson had written. That's why he had decided to write a letter himself in support of his friend. He dared to make the tone of his letter somewhat sharper. He would definitely let the board know that other mission organizations in China were appalled at the way in which they treated their employees. And that the British Bible Society was eager to work together with Hudson Taylor. Doctor Parker was happy that he was not dependent upon the CES organization, especially now that he would soon be a hospital doctor in Ningbo.

His pen flew over the paper.

* * *

In the meantime, Hudson walked down the stairs towards the cellar where he always prepared his medicines. "Today it must happen …" he murmured softly to himself. "I have thought about it long enough."

Already since his birthday he had been thinking about the idea of adapting more to the Chinese way of life. His servants had praised him then about how skilfully he could eat with chopsticks. They had asked him, "Why don't you wear our clothing? And why don't you braid your hair in a bianzi?"

He had smiled and said, "Having a blond braid would not make me a Chinese. After all, don't Chinese people have black braids?"

But he had thought about the idea more and more. Doctor Medhurst had also advised him to wear Chinese clothing, especially in the Chinese interior. Then there would be a greater chance that the Chinese people would accept him. Doctor Medhurst had experienced that himself.

He had bought Chinese clothing and today he was planning to make black paint to colour his blond hair. His hair was now long enough to be braided.

Carefully he arranged the substances he was going to mix on the work table. He took a mortar and pestle. Then he was ready to add the ammonia. However, the bottle was up quite high. Hudson stood on his toes and then he could just reach the big bottle with both hands. He was glad when it was standing on the work table. He carefully grabbed the cork between his thumb and index finger and cautiously tried to uncork the bottle. He knew like no one else did that he had to be very careful. He was doing a dangerous job because if the cork came off too quickly, the contents could spill over him and that could be deadly.

He was not having much success. His hands were wet with sweat. He decided to try once more. And then …

* * *

"Help, help!"

Doctor Parker jumped up, shaking with fright. What was going on? He heard the servants screaming. And … did he hear Hudson's voice also? He threw his crown pen on the writing table and ran downstairs! The noise was coming from the kitchen.

He held his breath when he saw what was happening there. Hudson Taylor was hanging with his head, shoulders and arms in the big water barrel. He sneezed as he came out of the water but immediately dove back in. The servants were running back and forth and screaming. Everyone was in a panic.

Doctor Parker was terrified when he saw that Hudson's face was completely swollen. He could hardly recognize him.

"Amm … monia," Hudson stammered.

Then Doctor Parker understood everything. Hudson Taylor had been burned!

"Keep rinsing with water. I'll be back in a minute!" he shouted.

He ran to the cellar as fast as he could. He grabbed a bottle of oil from the shelf, ran to the kitchen and immediately started to apply it all over Hudson.

"Here, Hudson. Especially on your eyes. That's important. I know it hurts but we have to do it!"

"Get me the opium," he commanded to one of the servants. He saw that Hudson could hardly bear the pain.

"Breathe in, Hudson," he ordered sternly. "Your life depends on it."

Hudson Taylor sniffed the opium with great difficulty. For a minute it seemed like he was losing consciousness. Doctor Parker and the servants carefully picked him up and put him on his bed.

"Make sure there is enough ice in the house," the doctor instructed. "It is of utmost importance that we keep Hudson cool. Not just for a bit, but today and tonight."

* * *

Irritated, Hudson Taylor put the letter he had just read on the table. It was a week after his accident. "More trouble," he said angrily. "So we have to leave this house shortly because it will be rented out to other future missionaries. The new renters are already on their way and we only just found out! How is that possible?"

Doctor Parker nodded. "That's the way it is, Hudson."

"I guess so. It is not a problem for you," Hudson grumbled. "You're leaving early tomorrow for Ningbo but I have to go and look for another place to stay. And where will I get the money?"

Doctor Parker looked directly at Hudson. Then he asked in a calm voice, "Hudson, has God ever disappointed you when there were problems? Has He not helped you in all your difficulties? And whom do you have to thank that your burn injuries healed so quickly? Would the same God not be mighty enough to find a house for you also this time?"

Hudson bowed his head in shame. His friend was right. He had to think of what Job said, "He shall deliver thee in six troubles: yea, in seven there shall no evil touch thee." He should not lose courage. It was true that it was extremely difficult to find an affordable house in Shanghai. But if this was God's plan, He would certainly find a solution.

"You know what?" Doctor Parker proposed, "How about you come along with me for some distance to my new residence in Ningbo. Let's say you travel along till Hangzhou Bay. Who knows what you may come across on the way?"

Suddenly Hudson felt new courage. What Doctor Parker proposed was not such a bad idea. You never knew what could happen. "I'll travel along with you for awhile tomorrow," he decided. "Thank you for your wise advice."

* * *

The next morning the Parker family and Hudson Taylor were sitting in the shabbily furnished kitchen of Doctor Medhurst's house. The sweet smell of jasmine tea hung in the air. The servants were busy packing the last pieces of baggage.

The Parkers had just admired Hudson Taylor's Chinese clothing. They respected him for wearing it because it was quite a step. Not all missionaries would appreciate that Hudson was doing this. But he was fully determined to follow through with it, although in reality he had no choice. A Chinese barber had painted his hair pitch black and braided it in a bianzi. The man would travel with Hudson for the coming days until Hudson was able to braid it himself.

They all felt a little sad. This would be their last breakfast together. A new future lay ahead of them all. What would it bring? They did not know, but God knew.

One of the servants knocked on the door and entered the kitchen. He bowed deeply. "Everything is ready, sir," he said politely.

Mr. Parker nodded to the others. "It's time to leave, friends."

17. A New Friend

1855-1856

December 2, 1855

Dear Mother,
My life has changed dramatically since Doctor Parker left for Ningbo. I miss my friends and their children. But I have to say that since they left I may clearly experience God's love. The Lord is good. Not only do I rent a house in Shanghai, but in the past weeks I have also rented a house on the island of Chongming (about sixty kilometres from Shanghai). A million people who have never heard of God live on that island. Thanks to my Chinese appearance, I am becoming more and more accepted by the people. I still have to get used to having a part of my head shaved. Oh, how the sun can burn on my head! I often use an umbrella like the natives to protect myself from the heat. I am getting better at braiding my hair with the silk ribbon. But walking on slippery Chinese shoes remains difficult. I am used to wearing the wide, loose-fitting pants. They don't look very nice but I gladly wear them because they help me to be more accepted by the Chinese population.

There are also less pleasant things to write about. Other doctors and pharmacists in Chongming have become jealous of my success. They have done everything they could to get rid of me. And they have succeeded. I was able to work here for six weeks but the British consul has urged me to leave; otherwise I will have to pay a fine of five hundred pounds. They say the reason is because I am renting a house outside the harbours where foreigners are allowed to rent. So I have to return to Shanghai. I leave the people here behind with pain in my heart. They still have so many questions. But the seed of God's Word has been sown here. That will remain behind here on the island. The Lord Himself will take care of the fruits.

But I have also happy things to tell you about. A young man wants to be baptized. I cannot tell you how much joy that gives me. I have sung, "My soul doth magnify the Lord, and my spirit hath rejoiced in God, my Saviour."

Dear Mother, don't worry about me too much. God has given me a new friend, Missionary William Burns. He is an older man and he gives me a lot of good advice. He is like a spiritual father to me. And I have received money again from Mr. William Berger from England. This gentleman has a heartfelt concern for mission work in China. In this way the Lord confirms His word, "Open thy mouth wide, and I will fill it."

Will you continue to pray for me?

Your loving son,
Hudson Taylor

* * *

It was still early in the morning. A grey plume of smoke slowly rose up through the clear sky above the river. The ship of Captain Bowers chugged between the high hills and terrace-like valleys.

"Look at the beautiful scenery," Hudson Taylor remarked to his friend William Burns, as the two stood on the after-deck.

"I have never seen such tall cactuses. And look at the palm trees and the other tropical trees!"

"It's really beautiful here. But unfortunately that cannot be said of the city of Shantou where we will be landing tomorrow. If it is true what Captain Bowers has told us, we will meet rough, uncivilized and corrupt Chinese people. A human life does not matter to them. The people live off opium and the trading of women and slaves."

"It is actually quite remarkable," Hudson said, "that we just met this Christian captain in Shanghai who offered to take us to Shantou for free. After all, it is a journey of eight hundred kilometres!"

"That is certainly true. But what I find so remarkable is that we were both deeply convinced that the Lord had called us to go there, even though we had not discussed it with each other."

"Indeed," Hudson smiled, "I was troubled by the thought that after three months I would have to say goodbye to you already. Therefore, I waited as long as possible to tell you that God had called me to go to Shantou."

"But I was glad that you started talking about it. Because I found it very difficult to have to go there by myself and to have to say goodbye to you."

"We are only insignificant people. We do not understand God. But if He calls us to go to such a corrupt city, I firmly believe that He will also have work for us to do there," Hudson said fervently. "I hope that I can write in my diary tomorrow: March 12, 1856. Arrival in Shantou."

* * *

It was not long before Hudson and William Burns found a place to live in Shantou. They tried to make contact with the people as quickly as possible. They travelled around the city every day.

"Go with God, Hudson," William said one day when Hudson told him that he wanted to go to a remote village among the hills.

"Thank you, Mr. Burns. I hope that I will be able to bring God's message to the people there. We will find out today what the result is of the intensive language lessons I took during the last few weeks. Well, if I cannot make myself understood, I hope that my servant can help me."

He flung a bag with tracts over his shoulder and crawled through the hole in the ceiling together with his helper. They stepped onto the rickety ladder and descended it one rung at a time.

Hudson and William had become completely used to their shabby place in Shantou. They did not mind that it was above an incense store. They preferred living among the poor Chinese people rather than living in the expensive part of the city where most of the foreigners lived. They felt at home here because there was room for the message of God's Word. Even in the incense store!

After walking for half an hour, Hudson and his servant saw the place they wanted to visit in the distance.

As soon as they entered the village, Hudson asked a passer-by, "Is there, perhaps, a school here? Or do you know a teacher who lives here?"

The older man answered gruffly, "We? A school and a teacher? We are far too poor to pay for something like that!" To prove his point, he pointed to his tattered, frayed pants.

Hudson looked the man straight in the eye and said, "Would you be this poor if you smoked less opium? Or if you gave less money to your idols? What have your offers and prayers given you? Have your idols heard you?"

There was a tense silence for a minute. More and more people gathered around Hudson and his helper. It was not long before forty people were crowded around them.

Suddenly an angry voice rang out, "This stranger is right. What good have our idols done for us? We live in utter poverty. There is nothing but trouble and sorrow here."

"But I know a God who is worthy to be honoured," Hudson Taylor said resolutely. "He is the God who created heaven and earth. And He cares for His creation every day. He has sent His Son to this world. We sin every day against this God but He is willing and able to forgive sin. He can also save you from the punishment we deserve. If you believe in this God, He will care for you in this life and also after this life."

The people stared at him in amazement.

"Which God do you honour?" they asked curiously.

"The God of heaven and earth. I have here the words of the God whom I serve. Who of you is able to read?"

Two people came forward.

"Here are some tracts and parts of the Word of God. Could you read this to the other villagers? I hope I will be able to come back another time to tell you more about this God."

The two men gratefully accepted the books.

Full of courage, Hudson and his helper continued on their way.

* * *

A few months later Hudson Taylor leaned over the railing of the ship *Wild Flower,* enjoying the quietness and coolness of the wind. He stared into the mirror-like water. How tired he was! The extreme heat of the past months had completely exhausted him. There had been times when it was so warm in Shantou that it seemed as if the sun was burning through the metal roof of their shabby room. They were often bothered by cockroaches, fleas and other insects.

Hudson shivered. Yes, sometimes it was difficult. Shantou was truly a corrupt city. He had often lain awake at night because he heard young women being assaulted in neighbouring houses. Oh, the need was very great. He fervently hoped that he would be able to return there soon.

Until now, he and William Burns had done a lot of work. As a result, many people had come into contact with the Gospel. He had also been able to help many sick people. The Lord had blessed his work. And they had been spared from attacks and crime.

But now he first had to go to Shanghai to get medicine for the Mandarin who had an incurable disease. No other doctor in Shanghai could help the Mandarin anymore, so he had asked Hudson if he could heal him.

Hudson quietly shook his head. No, he was unable to cure the Mandarin but God could bless the medicine that he was going to get in Shanghai for his benefit.

Hudson smiled a little bit. Sometimes he could not understand himself. The quietness on the boat was doing him a lot of good. And yet he was thankful that they were almost to Shanghai. In reality, he never really allowed himself to relax. There was still such a great need in China.

* * *

As soon as the ship had docked, Hudson was one of the first to get off. He walked straight to the warehouse where all his equipment and other important medicines were stored. He was curious what was left of his equipment. It would not be the first time that something had been stolen.

When he reached the office of the warehouse, he met with a painful surprise. He was very disappointed when the manager told him the message. An enormous fire had destroyed the warehouse. The part where his equipment and medicines were stored had also been destroyed by fire.

Tears welled up in Hudson's eyes. He needed the medicine more than ever before and now everything was gone. It was impossible to buy new medicines in Shanghai because they were far too expensive.

"Lord, help me," he stammered. "How can I continue? All these things are against me."

The words frightened him. It was as if he saw the apostle Paul in his thoughts standing in front of him. How many adversities he had experienced! And what did Paul say? "All things work together for good to them that love God ..."

Ashamed, Hudson folded his hands. "Lord," he prayed, "wilt Thou help me? Nothing is impossible with Thee."

He decided to go to Ningbo. Maybe his friend Doctor Parker, the hospital doctor, could get medicine for him!

18. Working in Ningbo

1856

An oppressive heat hung between the houses in the city of Ningbo. Many people had gone to the river to cool off, but two men were busily talking in the back garden of Doctor Parker.

"How glad I am, my friend," Doctor Parker said to Hudson Taylor, "that you are with us again. My wife and I have often wondered how you were doing. It is clear that we have many reasons to thank God. When I hear in what dangerous situations you have been in the crime-ridden city of Shantou, we can safely say that God has protected you. But it must have been quite a disappointment for you when you heard that all your equipment and medicines had gone up in flames in Shanghai."

"That's true. And I have not even told you everything," Hudson Taylor said cautiously, as he tried to cool himself off by waving a paper fan in front of him.

Doctor Parker looked at him inquisitively.

"As you know," Hudson continued, "I would have been able to reach Ningbo in three, or at the most four days, after having reached Shanghai on July 22. But God has led my way very differently. Because there was not enough water in the Grand Canal, the ship I had wanted to take to Ningbo could not sail and so I was forced to walk here. That took me three weeks. On the way I was able to preach and hand out tracts. But it was a journey with many difficulties. What do you think of my coolies who could not carry my baggage any farther because they said they were too tired? Apparently they were addicted to opium. And can you believe that Youxi, my faithful servant, robbed me?"

"Are you sure?" Doctor Parker interrupted him.

"Yes, it's really true. He stole two watches, my camera, my pictures, a few medical instruments, my harmonica and several expensive books about the Chinese language. I even lost my clothes. But I can handle all that. What I find worst of all is that I lost the Bible which my mother had given to me."

"Well," Doctor Parker said excitedly, "you must have gone immediately to court to report the theft? You must have demanded the return of your possessions?"

Hudson Taylor shook his head. "No, I did not do that on purpose. Would you like to know why? I have always prayed for the conversion of Youxi. If I would report him to the Mandarin, Youxi would end up in prison and he would never hear about Christ anymore. I could not bear that thought. Therefore, instead of reporting him, I sent him a personal letter. I told him that I will not report him because Christ has said, 'Overcome evil with good.'"

Doctor Parker felt a lump in his throat.

"Hudson," he said with a trembling voice, "you have dealt with him as Christ has dealt with those who persecuted Him. I am often too quick-tempered. May God bless your tolerance and patience."

The doctor closed his eyes for a minute. His good friend was sitting beside him, robbed and destitute. If only he could help him. Suddenly his eyes lit up. He had an excellent idea! He shot up and said, "Hudson, listen! I have a plan! Would you like to work for us? As the doctor on call I am responsible for the patients on the cargo ships. You could help me with that. And there is plenty of work at the new hospital which was built on the riverside outside the Salt Gate. In that way you could save up money for new medical equipment and medicines!"

Thankfully, Hudson looked at his friend. "If it is God's will, I will gladly do it!" he nodded.

* * *

The sun had barely risen when Hudson Taylor quietly closed the front door of Doctor Parker's house behind him. He wanted to start very early at the hospital this morning so that he could leave earlier in the afternoon. Then he would be able to preach on the terraces of the tea houses in the vast area of Ningbo, together with John Jones, his new friend who had been sent out by CES, just like him. Well, you could not really call it preaching because he first had to learn to improve his speaking of the Chinese dialect that was spoken in the area. But by going out with John and a missionary colleague named Gough, he had already learned to speak the dialect quite well.

But he did not speak it as well as Maria Dyer, the teacher of the first girls school that had been founded by missionaries. When he thought of her, a warm feeling filled his heart. Maria … he did not want others to know, but not a day went past that he did not think of her. She had made a deep impression on him right from the first time that he had seen her. She and her sister lived with Mrs. Aldersey, the woman who was the head of the girls school.

He would like to know what she thought of him. She was always cheerful and very friendly to him. But he wondered whether she could possibly have feelings of love for him.

He really enjoyed seeing her a few times a week. He was going to see her in two days again. Once a week Mrs. Aldersley and the two teachers had dinner with the Parker family. And it was very helpful that Maria was also friends with John and Mary Jones, so he saw her regularly at their place. Just as Hudson and John visited the villages outside Ningbo, Mary visited the Chinese women at their homes. By having tea with them she tried to talk to them about the Gospel. But she also did not speak the dialect well enough, so Maria accompanied her.

Hudson was certain of one thing: Maria Dyer would be an excellent wife for him! She also had a heart for mission work. Her own father had been a missionary for sixteen years. Sadly, both her parents had passed away in the meantime.

It was a pity that Mrs. Aldersey, who had more or less taken charge of Maria and Burella, was very bossy. She was a good headmistress but she was not an easy woman to deal with. She had let Hudson know in no uncertain terms that she thought it was nonsense that he wore Chinese clothing. And that letting his hair grow long and braiding it in a bianzi was totally wrong. Clearly, he could not expect anything positive from Mrs. Aldersey. She would certainly not give her permission for a relationship between him and Maria. In his thoughts he could easily picture Maria in front of him. She had beautiful, light-brown hair.

Hudson's arrival at the hospital brought an end to his pleasant thoughts.

* * *

Discouraged, Hudson Taylor was sitting in his new attic room above a classroom on Bridge Street at the end of a busy day. The room used to be rented out to his friend William Burns. Poor William. How would he be doing at this moment, Hudson wondered. He had just received a letter from him — from prison! Together with two other Chinese colleagues, William had been arrested and imprisoned by the Mandarin. That's why William had seriously warned him not to come to Shantou. At the moment it was very dangerous there, especially for foreigners.

But what did God want him to do if he did not return to Shantou? Did he have to stay here in Ningbo until God showed him another way? Did he just have to continue to care for children in the classroom and to provide poor people with food? It was true that about forty to seventy people who would otherwise perish from hunger came every day. In the evening they used the classroom as their church room. So they also had a hunger for God's Word. No, at the moment the problem was not that he had nothing to do. But he wanted so badly to reach more people in China. China was bigger than just Ningbo.

He no longer had any financial worries. Mr. Berger from England had just sent him another sixty pounds. From that money he had been able to buy all the medicines and medical equipment he needed. So he actually did not have to stay in Ningbo to work and earn money.

For a moment, the troubled feeling that he had experienced lately came over him again. He asked himself if he still felt at home here. He had noticed that other missionaries were asked more often than him to lead the services. It bothered him a lot. Why did they do that?

After all, he had more than three years of experience as a missionary and he was fluent in several Chinese dialects. And yet he felt that he was often passed over. Could the reason be that he had not finished his medical studies?

Hudson wiped the sweat off his forehead. He was tired and in a sombre mood. It seemed as if everything was against him. Mrs. Aldersey was becoming more negative towards him all the time. How would things ever work out between him and Maria? He loved her more and more but the question was whether she could ever become his wife. In his thoughts he could hear Mrs. Aldersey saying, "First of all, make sure that you are able to provide for a family, Mr. Hudson." And actually, she was right. Very occasionally he received money from his mission organization but that was too little to provide for a family. But where else could he go? Which mission organization wanted to accept someone who had not finished his medical studies? Would it be better if he returned to England to finish his studies first? He knew for certain that he did not want to stay for a long time with the mission organization which had sent him out. Especially not after he had heard from a reliable source that they borrowed money to pay the salaries of the missionaries. Is that what he wanted? Absolutely not. Would God not be mighty enough to care for them?

Restlessly, Hudson moved his chair back, got up and started to pace back and forth in his room. What did his future hold? He did not know anymore. Would he maybe have to give up all the mission work and become an ordinary doctor in England?

His eyes wandered along the walls until … his eye fell on two papyrus rolls. "Ebenezer," it said on one of the rolls. "Hitherto hath the Lord helped us." And on the other roll it said, "Jehovah Jireh, the Lord will provide."

Suddenly he felt ashamed. Oh, how it hurt him that he acted as if he had to solve all his problems. Did he have so little trust in God? Had the Lord ever left him to himself?

"Lord," he said softly, "forgive me and wilt Thou please strengthen my faith!"

19. Joy and Sorrow

1858

April 15, 1858

Dear Mother,

Solomon wrote, "Whoso findeth a wife findeth a good thing." I fully agree. I am so happy with Maria. I often think back to our wedding day, January 20, 1858. What a miracle that God Himself — despite all the obstacles against our marriage — has brought Maria and I together. I find it such a pity that you were not able to see her for yourself. She was such a beautiful bride in her simple grey gown with a veil.

Only now do I understand why the Lord took care that I could not leave Ningbo. It was to bring Maria and I together! Unfortunately, I have been sick for some time. That's why you have not heard from me for a few weeks. Thankfully I'm doing better now. At first Maria developed typhus at the end of our honeymoon. Together with Mary Jones, the wife of my friend John, I took care of her. During the first few weeks she did not improve at all but now she feels much better. After that I became ill. Now we can take care of ourselves again with the help of a few friends. Oh mother, I cannot tell you how much I love Maria. We are very happy in our little house on Bridge Street. We renovated the house here and there. The floors have been redone and we bought Chinese furniture. There is also a pharmacy so that I can take care of the opium addicts. In the evening I hold an evangelizing service if possible. In short, there is work enough in China.

But ... I have even much greater news. If everything goes well, you will have a grandchild after some time. Will you pray for Maria and the unborn child, Mother? Will you beg the Lord that He will make all things well? Greet Father, Amelia and Louisa from us also.

Your son and daughter-in-law,
Hudson and Maria

* * *

It was breathlessly quiet in the church room on Bridge Street in Shanghai. A small group of men were sitting in the twilight and listening to the story that Hudson Taylor was telling. They listened very intently. The oppressive heat did not bother them at all. Even the pesky mosquitoes, which came in through the open windows, could not distract them from paying attention.

The missionary told them of a son who had asked for his inheritance and then left his good father. Once he was far away from home, he led a wicked life. It was not long before his money was gone. He almost perished with hunger. Yes, the men knew very well what hunger was!

The boy decided to go back to his father. Everything was much better at home. But ... would his father still be willing to have him back?

In their thoughts they saw the father standing with his hand above his eyes, staring into the distance to see if his son was coming back home. And when this son did come back, his father lovingly embraced him! The people in the room could not understand it at all.

"In this way God waits for people like you and me, for people who have walked away from Him." Hudson concluded his story, "God is still gracious. He gave His Son, the Lord Jesus Christ, for such people."

It was quiet for a moment. Suddenly Nyi Yongfa stood up and confessed with tears, "People, I think most of you know me. I am a cotton merchant. I have been seeking the truth for years. I have been the leader of a Buddhist sect. I have not been able to find rest anywhere. But what I have learned tonight is the truth. I firmly believe that! I can feel it in my heart. From now on I believe in the Lord Jesus Christ!"

Deeply impressed, the people left the church room that evening.

Hudson Taylor was astonished. God was working! More people had come to faith in the last while. Dang, the basket maker, and Tsiu, the teacher, and his mother. But also Wang, the farmer. And Wang Lae-djun, the painter. They had promised to spread the Gospel among their people. They wanted to spend their lives in the service of the Gospel. Would Nyi also want to join this group?

Hudson did not have to wait long for an answer. As soon as the others had left, Nyi came towards him and asked, "Sir, could you come along with me once to visit the sect of which I was the leader until recently? I want to tell them that there is a God in heaven who saves people."

"Of course I'm willing to do that," Hudson Taylor promised, pleasantly surprised. "Let me know when you would like to go."

"Thank you, sir," Nyi answered politely, bowing deeply. "And may I take a New Testament along? I would like to study God's Word."

* * *

A few days later they were on their way to visit the Buddhist sect. Suddenly Nyi Yongfa asked, "Sir, may I ask you a strange question? How long has the Gospel been known in England?"

Surprised, Hudson Taylor looked at the cotton merchant for a minute but then he understood the question. "For a few hundred years already, Nyi," he said cautiously.

"But, sir, why did the people of England never come to us sooner to tell us that it is possible to be saved? My father searched for the truth for more than twenty years but he never found it. He died without hope ..."

The words touched Hudson Taylor deeply. He bowed his head in shame. How long his people had left the Chinese people ignorant of salvation! Suddenly he knew for certain: he had to stay in China. Not only as a doctor or pharmacist, but much more importantly to win souls for Christ. He felt again the great need of the Chinese people. He could not do this great work alone. Many more missionaries had to come. Every day thousands of Chinese people died who had never heard of the One Name whereby they could be saved!

* * *

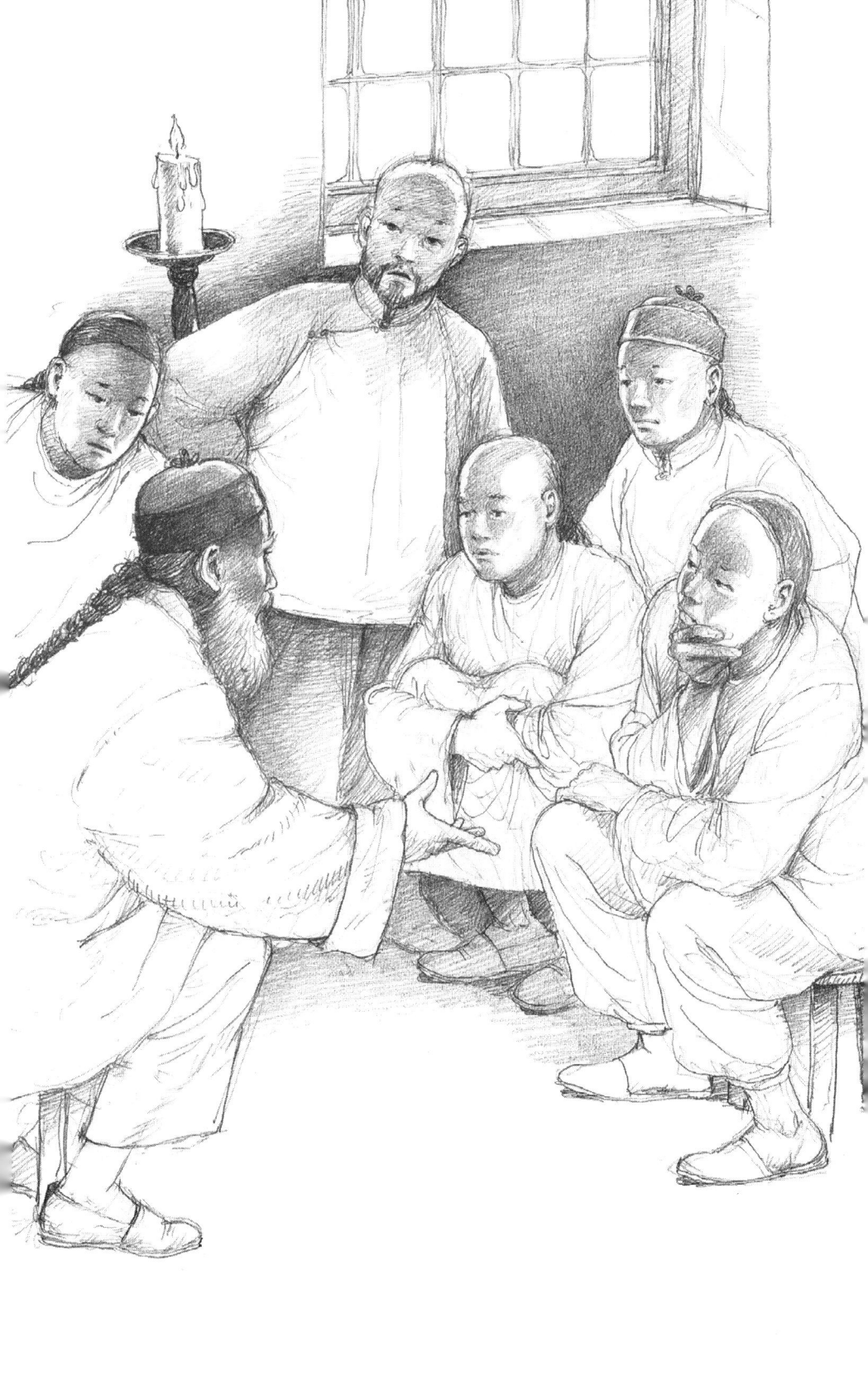

October 1858

Dear Mother,

We have something very sad to tell you. Hudson has asked me to let you know. Our little baby, whom we had been expecting for seven months, died at birth. It was taken home by God. We are very sad, but not without hope. God knows how much you and we have prayed for this child. Will you please pray that God will keep us from having rebellious thoughts? We have so many reasons to be thankful. More and more people are coming to conversion here. We have even established a small congregation. The people have to sacrifice much to be a Christian in word and deed. Sundays are especially a problem. Then they are not allowed to work according to God's law, but that means that they don't earn anything. For that reason some don't want to join the congregation because Hudson is very strict on this point. Thankfully, there are also people who are willing to make "sacrifices" for this.

We also have evening classes now where people are learning how to read the New Testament. God is good. We still receive so many blessings. He also knows why our child died so young. Greet everyone from us.

Your loving daughter-in-law Maria

20. A God of Miracles

1859

On Sunday, July 31, excited voices could be heard in the streets of Ningbo. For days the city had been gripped by a terrible tension. A scorching heat of forty degrees was making the blood of the Chinese population pulse even faster through their veins. They were outraged. What did these foreigners think? That they could take advantage of them? That they would allow their children to be taken and sold as coolies?

The population wanted only one thing and that was revenge. Away with all these foreigners in China!

Occasionally they expressed their anger by pounding on the door of these foreigners. It was also noisy on Bridge Street.

From time to time Hudson Taylor peeked outside through a crack in the curtains of his bedroom. His only hope was in the Lord. He and Maria stood powerless. The only means to save them was a boat which lay ready by the back door in case they had to flee. And a rope hung from the bedroom window, which they could use to let themselves down in case of an emergency. But they could not use these means of escape because the baby could be born any minute.

Hudson softly spoke words of encouragement to Maria.

He heard the people in the room downstairs singing. There was a service being led by his friend John Jones. Oh, Hudson knew for sure that they would certainly pray for Maria and the child which was to be born. That gave him courage.

His thoughts went back to last February. Then Maria had been at the brink of death. He had truly thought that he would lose her. While he had been on his way to the hospital to ask Doctor Parker for advice, the Lord had powerfully spoken these words to him, "And call upon Me in the day of trouble: I will deliver thee, and thou shalt glorify Me." It was a miracle that he had received Maria back. Since that time the text had meant much to him. Also today. He could not flee with his pregnant wife. And yet there was peace in his heart. After all, God was faithful and He always did what He promised.

Outside, a shrill voice yelled, "Death to the foreign devils." Inside, Mary Jones, who was ready to be the midwife, nodded meaningfully at Hudson. It was time for the baby to be born. No one cared about what was happening outside. A short while later, Hudson Taylor held his little daughter in his arms.

"Maria," he said, deeply moved, "I have always longed and prayed that I would be able to hold a little girl, who looks like you, in my arms. God has heard my prayers. Here is our little Grace Dyer Taylor!"

* * *

It was a few weeks later. Bewildered, Hudson and Maria looked at their friend Doctor Parker, who sat dejectedly in front of them. They could hardly believe that what he had just told them was true. They were still completely filled with the miracle of the birth of little Grace. Their little girl was now three weeks old. Whereas there was so much joy in their house, a great sorrow had entered the house of Doctor Parker. His wife had suddenly died from cholera.

Doctor Parker wrung his hands and stared at the floor. He did not know how to continue. How could he, as a man, look after his four children? The last five years he had been very busy with his work as a doctor in the hospital, and with his own private clinic, which was running very well. He felt as if he were at the end of his strength. Besides, one of his children was seriously ill. Therefore, he had decided to return to his parents in Scotland with his family as soon as possible. However, his big question was about what to do with the hospital and the patients. He would have liked to transfer the responsibility to Hudson, but where would he get the necessary money to keep it running?

"I think, Hudson," Doctor Parker mused, "that we have to close the hospital with its fifty beds. I hate to do it, but I see no other way. How can you pay the staff and everything that is needed to keep it running? You can count on it that the daily costs and the medicines for the patients and the staff will be very high."

Hudson drew some random figures on the floor with his soft shoes. Many thoughts went through his mind. Would the hospital have to be closed because there was not enough money? Had God not promised, "And whatsoever ye shall ask in My name, that will I do"? Had this God ever put him to shame? No, never! "With God's help I would like to take the responsibility for the hospital and the pharmacy upon me," he said resolutely. "I may not give up my trust in Him. I am unwilling and unable to do that."

* * *

Hudson did not want to waste any time. The next day he immediately called the whole staff together in one of the hospital's rooms. He told them honestly that he was not sure if he would be able to pay their wages in the future, as Doctor Parker had been able to do.

"Tell me," he asked, "will you put your trust in God in the future? Or do you not dare to do that?"

There was an uncomfortable silence for a minute. Hudson looked directly at the employees. Soon a few assistants came forward and told him that they wanted to accept his proposal. After that more followed. There were also a few employees who indicated that they did not want to work under these conditions. But thankfully, there were not many like that.

Hudson left the hospital that day with a thankful heart. He was firmly convinced that with God's help he would succeed!

* * *

It was several weeks later. Hudson stood speechless, looking into the envelope which had just been delivered. It was unbelievable! The envelope contained fifty pounds! It had again been sent by the well-known Mr. Berger from England. Since this man had read about the robbery by Youxi in *The Harvester*, he had sent money several times. Last year Hudson had already received just over 300 pounds from him. Tears welled up in his eyes as he continued reading. Mr. Berger's father had died and had left a lot of money to his son. Mr. Berger wanted to spend the money in the service of God's Kingdom. He wrote, "If you need more money in China, please let me know ..."

Hudson went to find his wife as fast as he could. "Maria," he said, full of emotion, "do you remember that our cook told us a few days ago that he had started to use the last bag of rice? Now see what we have received! Fifty pounds!"

Maria put her hands in front of her mouth in amazement.

"Is it really true, Hudson?" she exclaimed.

"Yes, it is really true. And it shall come to pass that before they call, I will answer, the Lord has promised. Our workers have prayed every day since we became responsible for the hospital and the clinic. I am deeply convinced that this is an answer to our prayers."

That day the news of the miracle of the large amount that Hudson had received spread like wildfire through the hospital. The patients were also speechless. The God of the foreigners was a God of miracles!

21. Back to England

1860

"If we could find five more people, Maria, we would be able to tell many more Chinese people about the Gospel in the future." Hudson sighed as he stared into the endless distance through the small, round window. He saw nothing but water and more water. Together with Maria, he was sitting in their cabin on board the *Jubilee*. The sun's rays reflected off the smooth blue sea. China was a few days of sailing behind them. They hoped to arrive in England in a few months. Maria nodded in agreement. "I know, Hudson," she said quietly, "but try to distance yourself from your work a little bit. We did not leave China for nothing. You badly need your rest! Daily we ask God if we may find five people in England who are will to return to China as missionaries. Have a little bit of trust. At this moment it is especially important that you regain your strength. You have worked too hard after Doctor Parker left Ningbo. It is no wonder that your body is protesting. Don't forget that in the meantime you have also acquired tuberculosis."

"It is a very difficult situation, Maria," Hudson groaned wearily. "The fact that in the end we still had to close the hospital … It was a mission post in itself. The patients to whom we could speak about the Lord Jesus could in turn pass on the message of the Gospel to their families. In that way we were able to reach so many people. And all that has now ended …"

"That's true. But God has many more possibilities. For instance, you took our Chinese friend Wang Lae-djun along on our trip. The two of you want to translate Christian reading material and hymns into Chinese during the next little while. Do you not sow the seed of the Word of God in that way as well? At the moment you feel useless but maybe God has completely different thoughts about that. He must have a reason that you had to give everything up. We do not understand it, but God is always in control."

Hudson reflected on what Maria had said. It was about seven years ago that he had left for China. For as long as he could remember, he had daily felt the need of millions of people who lived without God. That need weighed even heavier on him now than it had back then. Just before they had embarked on the *Jubilee* in Shanghai to sail to England, he had written to Amelia, "If I had a thousand pounds, I would give them to China. If I had a thousand lives, China could ask for every one of them. Oh no, not China, but the Lord Jesus. Because we can never do too much or even enough for Him."

"You are right, Maria," Hudson finally admitted. "It is indeed very difficult to follow. And yet the Lord is good. Seven years ago I left for China by myself. And now I may return with you and Grace."

"Shh ..." Maria warned. "Do I hear our little girl? Maybe she is awake." She quickly got up and walked to the adjacent cabin.

* * *

"Come and have a look! Hudson is here!"

Louisa's high-pitched voice resounded through the stately house on Westbourne Grove in London on Tuesday, November 20, 1860. She was dancing for joy in the door opening.

As Amelia and her husband Benjamin came to see what all the commotion was about, Louisa was already in her brother's arms.

"Hudson!" she exclaimed. "Is it you?"

She held him at a distance for a minute. Hudson looked very strange in his Chinese clothing and his hair was in an odd, long braid down his back.

"Louisa," said Hudson.

Then she knew for sure. It was really her brother. She wrapped her arms around him again.

Maria smiled as she stood on the sidewalk with little Grace. How happy Louisa and Amelia were to see their brother again!

Wang Lae-djun could not believe his eyes. Did the family of Hudson and Maria live in this big house? He found it difficult to cope with all that he was seeing. First of all, he had found the train ride from the harbour city of Gravesend to London very exciting. He had never been in a train in his entire life. And did he have to stay in the big house on this fashionable street? But he did not have much time to think about it all.

"Come on in," Benjamin said. "Welcome to our home."

As Amelia served tea to the guests, the stories started. Louisa was horrified when she heard that the beds on the ship were full of fleas. And that they all had been sick at sea!

"I'm glad the voyage only took four months this time, " Hudson said, smiling. "In the end we landed safely. And, dear Amelia and Benjamin, we are extremely grateful that we may stay here for the next while. It is quite something for you. Especially because Maria is expecting our second child."

* * *

With a worried expression Doctor Clarke looked at the patient who had come into his office with all kinds of complaints. The ashen color of his face and his sunken cheeks clearly indicated that the man across from him had taxed himself to the limit during the last while. He had worked day and night for almost seven years in China in the most impoverished circumstances. He remembered from before that Hudson had already been very driven and hard-working as a student. But this task in China had been too demanding for him.

Doctor Clarke had just examined Hudson. He had been in England on furlough for just over two months now. But he was not doing very well. This furlough would possibly have to last for a long time.

Doctor Clarke wondered how he should tell Hudson about his health. He concluded from what the missionary had just told him, that his heart was still in China. The doctor did not want to discourage him too much.

"Hudson," he said, as he drummed his fingers on the edge of the desk, "I'm afraid I have to disappoint you. You have enough medical knowledge yourself to be able to understand that you cannot really return to China with a damaged liver and an upset digestive tract.

Certainly not in the short term. It is clear that your nerves have been strained. I urgently advise you against returning to Ningbo shortly. It could cost your life."

Hudson stared at his former teacher in astonishment. "But ... but are you really serious, Doctor Clarke?" he stammered. "May I not return to China? That's impossible!"

"Alas, Hudson, I am serious. Listen to me and do what I tell you. Forget about making any trip abroad for some time. And ... maybe I have to say that you should forget about it permanently."

Hudson felt crushed as he left the massive hospital in London.

"Never back to China," were the words that reverberated through his head. "Maybe never back to China ..." And that when things were not going very well at all in Ningbo. He had received a letter from John and Mary Jones. They wrote that the young congregation was struggling.

Hudson felt intensely sad. Could he leave his sick "children" behind by themselves? Discouraged, he lifted up his hands towards heaven and stammered, "Lord, what is going to happen?"

Then it was as if the Lord pointed him to the fact that not he, but the Lord Himself would take care of His children. He showed Hudson that He was the Good Shepherd, who had bought His sheep with His own blood. It was as if a voice in his heart said at the same moment: "He shall feed His flock like a shepherd: He shall gather the lambs with His arm, and carry them in His bosom, and gently lead those that are with young."

"I thank Thee, Lord!" Hudson said softly. "I have to remember that. All things are secure in Thy hands!"

22. Praying and Working for China

1864-1866

With a deep sigh Hudson Taylor closed the ink pot and pushed it to the side of the desk. He was pleased. Carefully he put the pen back down in its holder.

His eyes restlessly wandered around the room. The article that had to be handed in tomorrow to one of the many magazines was finally finished. His eyes rested on the map directly across from his desk. There were still eleven provinces in China that had not been visited by missionaries. Millions of people died there without ever having heard of God! The thought made him feel discouraged.

Since his return to England, he had first finished his medical studies. Then he had obtained the midwifery diploma. Assisted by Maria and Wang Lae-djun, he had translated hymns and the New Testament into the Ningbo dialect. But that did not help those millions of people. It had not changed the desperate situation in China.

God had provided four of the five missionaries for whom they had prayed all along. Two young people, James and Martha Meadows, had left for China in January of 1862, along with William Parker who had remarried after the death of his wife. But Hudson could not understand God's way anymore. Doctor Parker, who was known as one of the best missionaries in China, had only been able to work there for a short time. During one of his trips he had fallen off his horse and landed in the frigid water of the river. It had cost him his life. In the meantime, Martha Meadows had died from cholera. And John Jones, one of his best friends with whom he had worked so often in China, had died at sea during his return trip to England.

It seemed as if everything were going wrong.

Dejectedly Hudson walked to the window. What did God want to tell him with all these trials?

In a few days, on December 20, 1864, the fifth missionary, an intelligent young woman named Jean Norman, would be leaving for

China. He would have liked to accompany her to encourage his friends and the people there. But he realized he was unable to go along. He often wrestled with the problem that he and Maria, together with the other workers, could only reach a very small portion of the population with the Gospel. He was becoming more and more convinced that five mission workers were definitely not enough. At least two people would be needed for each of the eleven provinces that did not have a missionary yet. He would like to beg God for a total of twenty-four missionaries. And yet ... he did not do that. Not that he doubted that God was mighty enough to make so many people willing. He was firmly convinced that He could. But his big question was: Who would carry the responsibility for all those people? He could not expect anything from the mission organization which had sent him out. It had been discontinued. He and Maria did not dare to take on the responsibility for twenty-four missionaries. Imagine if the mission workers met with disappointments? What would he do then? He knew beforehand that everything would not be easy for them. Take the journey to China, for instance. Would they accept the fact that they would have to suffer hunger, or that they could become seriously ill and so on? Or would they blame him for everything because he had persuaded them to go?

Hudson was starting to feel anxious. For a minute it was as if he could not breathe. Oh, he was not willing; he was not able. And yet ... God said, "If thou forbear to deliver them that are drawn unto death!"

* * *

Hudson Taylor banged his fist down on the book he had just completed. It was lying in front of him on the table.

"What did you think? Why did I write this book?"

Before his two friends William Berger and George Pearce could answer, he continued. "Because no mission organization dares to accept the responsibility of sending out missionaries. With this book I want to shake the English people awake. I want to point out to them their responsibility. How can they let all those millions of Chinese people go lost?"

Berger and Pearce nodded in agreement. Hudson was right! All three of them completely agreed that a special mission organization had to be established to reach the interior of China. But how?

"We don't need people who have studied at a university. Definitely not. We need practical, believing Christians. They will mean a lot in the service of the Kingdom of God," Hudson continued. "I hope we will get people who have enough courage to take on this task. I hope we will get people who feel that they are dependent on God's help and direction. We need people who do not expect it from us or from each other, but only from God. And then not only men, but also women. They are the ones who can visit the Chinese women at home."

As Hudson tried to emphasize his words with forceful gestures, beads of sweat stood out on his brow.

Deeply concerned, William Berger and George Pearce looked at their friend.

"Hudson," George said anxiously, "are you alright? Would it not be better for you if you took a break? Are you not taking on too much?"

Hudson felt confused. He nodded. "You are right, George," he answered humbly. "I have hardly been able to sleep for the last few months. I usually sleep only one hour a night. In my thoughts, I am busy with China day and night. I am telling you all this because I don't want to trouble Maria with it. She is busy enough with our four children."

"I understand," William nodded. "But you cannot continue like this any longer."

"Just a minute ... I have a proposal," George suggested. "Why don't you come to our place in Brighton for the weekend from June 24 to 26? I think that a few days of rest would be very good for you."

"I am completely exhausted," Hudson admitted in a listless voice. "Maybe it will be good to take a break. I gladly accept your proposal. Thank you, George!"

* * *

It was a beautiful, calm Sunday morning in June. A lone man with bowed shoulders was walking on the beach of Brighton. It seemed as if he was carrying a heavy burden. It was Hudson Taylor.

As the waves rolled over the white beach in a steady rhythm, it was storming in his heart. He had just left the church full of anguish. At least a thousand people had been sitting there, quietly listening to the sermon, while millions of people in China were going lost because they did not know that God's Word existed! He could not cope with it anymore.

A fierce, spiritual struggle was raging in his heart. For months he had wrestled with the question whether he was willing to give guidance to twenty-four missionaries who would be sent to China. He firmly believed that God was able and willing to give so many mission workers. He also was not worried about the financial means. William Berger had promised to help him. But Hudson was still not willing to commit himself to the project.

Therefore, he intentionally did not pray for so many missionaries, even though he knew that thousands of people were going lost every day. He felt torn inside. He was unable; he did not dare, and yet God was asking him to …

"If thou forbear to deliver them that are drawn unto death!"

Startled, Hudson looked around. Again he had heard those same words! But it was not a person who had said these words to him. It was God's voice!

At the same moment he felt all his resistance break down. He did not want to oppose God any longer.

"Lord," he called out, "I surrender myself to Thee and Thy service. I may lay all responsibility at Thy feet. I only need to follow Thee as a servant to obey! Not I, but Thou carriest the responsibility. Thou art the God of heaven and earth. Wilt Thou look after twenty-two missionaries for the eleven provinces and two missionaries for Tartaria and Tibet?"

As he prayed, he felt that an enormous burden had been lifted off his shoulders. A profound peace filled his heart. He was walking on

the beach, alone with God. All his worries had disappeared! The whole creation smiled at him ...

Joyfully he took his Bible, grabbed a pencil out of his pocket and wrote at the place where he had finished reading, "Prayed for twenty-four willing, able workers, in Brighton, June 25, 1865."

As he slowly read the words again he notice to his surprise that he had written them above the text, "Oh, that my words were now written! Oh that they were printed in a book! That they were graven with an iron pen and lead in the rock forever!" (Job 19:23&24)

Two days later, on June 27, 1865, Hudson Taylor and George Pearce opened a bank account for their new foundation, the China Inland Mission, which would labour to bring the Gospel to the interior of China.

* * *

"What a special evening," one of the ladies whispered after Hudson Taylor's last words had echoed through the church in the district of Totteridge in North London. "It's amazing how this man can talk about China!"

Her words were drowned out by the deep voice of Colonel John Puget.

"Dear ladies and gentlemen, tonight you have heard about the great need in China. Mr. Taylor has shown us our responsibility. What are you doing for China? He has emphatically told me to include in the announcements that there will not be a collection at the end of the service, but I would like to propose that we still do it this time. The new China Inland Mission, or CIM, can certainly use the money. Mr. Taylor, I hope you have no objections against that?"

Hudson Taylor looked at the colonel. He felt somewhat annoyed. What was going on? He and his family and friends had organized meetings everywhere in England and Scotland. People knew that these meetings had not been organized to collect money but to make everyone aware of the need in China!

"Dear Colonel," he answered, "I would like to stick to our agreement. It is not my intention to have people give their money in an emotional spur of the moment. What is important is that all the people present here tonight take the need for China home. Ask the Lord what He asks of you. Maybe He asks submission of you, or maybe He asks to have your child for mission work. There is a greater need for people who want to follow Christ than for money. I may tell you that our foundation, which has just been set up, is receiving a lot of money. And not because we go around telling everyone about our mission, but because God hears our prayers!"

* * *

The next morning Hudson was having an early breakfast. He was waiting for the colonel and wondering where he was. Then he heard footsteps in the hallway.

"Excuse me for being late," the colonel said as an apology. "I … I slept terribly last night."

"Is that so?" Hudson asked as the colonel joined him at the table.

"Indeed. And … um … I have to tell you something, Mr. Taylor." He was clearly searching for words. "Last night … I … had planned to give you five pounds but I kept thinking about it and I hardly slept all night. I'm not at peace with it. May I give you five hundred pounds? Please, will you accept the money?" he pleaded.

"If you are willing to give the money to the Lord and His service, I'll gladly accept it," Hudson answered happily. "It is not about me, or about us, or about the China Inland Mission. What is important is that we give our money out of love to God and our neighbour. And I am deeply convinced that God will certainly bless it if we give it like that."

A few hours later the mailman delivered an envelope at the colonel's house.

"It is for your guest, Mr. Taylor," he told the servant.

When the colonel put the letter in front of Hudson Taylor, he looked up in surprise. A letter for him?

He quickly opened the envelope. Then his eyes opened wide in surprise.

"Listen, Colonel. Do you know what it says here? This is an offer for a ship, the *Lammermuir*. It is a ship that is nicely equipped. I would be able to rent it for a group of missionaries who want to leave for China after May 20, 1866!"

The colonel listened to the message in amazement. How was it possible? Just at the right moment.

"What a beautiful offer," Hudson called out. "I just received exactly that amount from you. We can use the money to pay for the journey of the first twenty-four missionaries. Did you notice? God confirms His word, 'And it shall come to pass, that before they call, I will answer!' In China I had two sayings hanging on the wall: 'Jehovah Jireh' and 'Ebenezer'. I would like to add a third: 'Jehovah Nissi, the Lord is my Banner.'"

23. Back to China

1866-1867

"Go ahead and loosen the ropes, sailors!" the helmsman on the *Lammermuir* shouted. "The wind is picking up."

"He is right," one of the sailors pointed out. "Should we just …?"

Two men started to turn the enormous crank as quickly as possible. It was not long before the bulging sails flapped in the wind.

"Talking about the group of missionaries that we have on board …" the youngest sailor said. "I think there is something strange about them. Sixteen people plus a family are going to China! What are they thinking? They don't even know if they'll have a place to stay in Shanghai. They don't know how they will be able to get money. And they even think they will be able to go into the interior. Poor women! They will soon find out that they are not welcome over there."

"Yes, I don't understand everything either," the older sailor said cautiously, "but they are people who are doing it out of conviction. Take for example their leader, Hudson Taylor, and his wife. They know very well what they are getting into. They have lived in China for several years. And now they are going back with their four children."

The youngest sailor burst out laughing. "And a harmonium," he grinned. "Have you ever heard of someone taking a harmonium to China? I can just picture it. Litters and wheelbarrows are the only means of transportation in Shanghai. I hope that their harmonium does not need to be transported over the Garden Bridge because it is so narrow that two wheelbarrows can hardly pass each other."

"I'm sure they hope so, too, but still … what Hudson told us during the church service on Sunday impressed me. And not just me, because I have also heard others say the same thing. You know … I wish I had such a faith!"

"Are you serious?"

"Yes, I am. This group of people that we have on board have something that we miss! Deep in my heart I admire these missionaries and their leader. They give their lives to the service of their God. You can see that they are not afraid of the future at all. On the contrary. They study the Bible every day; they learn Chinese and they study the customs over there. They give everything for the service of God and their neighbour."

The youngest sailor casually shrugged his shoulders.

"Let me tell you this," his older mate continued. "It touched me deeply how they said farewell to their family and friends on May 26. Do you remember how they prayed together on the back deck? And how reverently they sang when we passed through the locks of the harbour?"

His voice quivered.

"Yes, my boy. I will never forget that."

The young sailor looked at him with a strange expression. His mate was deeply moved! He even had tears in his eyes! He was not used to hearing things like that from him. Maybe he should also go and listen to what this Hudson Taylor had to say on Sunday morning.

* * *

"We should not let these difficulties discourage us, Maria," Hudson Taylor said on a beautiful summer evening in August.

"Try to enjoy the beautiful scenery here. Look at those beautiful, bright hills. You're just exhausted because of the extreme heat that has hit the city during the last few weeks. That's all. I hope that you'll be able to relax a little bit here and I am convinced that then you'll start to feel better. And we won't go to the other missionaries in Hangzhou until you feel well again. Difficulties should make us more determined!" Tiredly Maria looked at her husband. Hudson was right. The Lord had helped them thus far. But she felt so very tired.

She stared ahead of her. Her thoughts went back to the last year, September 1866. They had landed in Shanghai with a damaged ship, despite the terrible storms which they had experienced. God had provided them with a place to live. That same day, Mr. Gable had offered them his warehouse to store their possessions. Shortly after that, in November, God had provided them a house with thirty rooms in Hangzhou. The house had everything that was needed for such a group of missionaries and for the work they did. Every day about two hundred people came to the clinic. Hudson was able to preach there every day. The other missionaries were also doing well. Each of them had found a place to work and they were being accepted by the Chinese population. A large reason for that was that they had adopted the lifestyle and the clothing of the Chinese people as much as possible. Actually, everything was going well and yet … she was so tired.

"I have the feeling, Hudson, that everything is becoming too much for me."

"Try to let things go a little bit, Maria. Our lives and our work are in God's hand. We have submitted our plans to Him. I still think that the most sensible step for the future is to first establish a congregation in the capitals. After that we can open posts in the cities of government. And finally we will allow the evangelists whom we have educated to go to the villages. When the people there see that the Mandarins in the cities give us their approval, they will decide to allow us into their villages even more quickly. I'm sure everything will turn out well. Look how God has taken care of us! And a new group of missionaries has already arrived in Hangzhou."

"That's true … but it makes me sad that one of our missionaries has already died this spring, Hudson," Maria countered.

"Yes, that also shocked me deeply. That's true. But God also wants to test our new foundation, the China Inland Mission. This trial will make us stronger, thanks to God's grace. And … we have to continue to count our blessings. At the beginning of the year God gave us a lovely daughter who carries your name. Is that not a great blessing? He already gave us two girls and three boys! May we say that we have lacked anything since our departure from England last May?"

* * *

September 1867,

Dear Mother,

I don't know how to tell you this. I have to tell you something very sad. God has taken our little Grace to Himself. While we were temporarily renting a house in the hills because Maria was not feeling well (it is very hot in the city at the moment), Grace contracted meningitis.

It started with vomiting and a high fever. The second day her speech was confused. We still put cold compresses on her face but it did not help. Four days later she contracted pneumonia. Grace died on Friday evening, August 23, at twenty minutes to nine.

Mother, we will never hear her lovely voice again. I will never feel her hand in my hand again as she always did when she came along with me. I wrote to William Berger on August 15 when I sat at her deathbed, 'My flesh and my heart faileth: but God is the strength of my heart, and my portion for ever.' And I still say that. We have been able to give our child back to our Heavenly Father. I am thankful that God took her unto Himself, even though she was like the sun in our lives. I am glad for her that she may now be eternally happy. Pray for us, Mother. Maria is doing a little bit better, but sometimes I find it difficult to cope with everything. The many worries about the work and the worries about the family. And yet I want to continue to believe in Him who has said, 'I will not fail thee, nor forsake thee. My strength is made perfect in weakness.'

Your loving son,
Hudson

24. A Deep Trial

1868-1870

"Maria, today I have spread before the Lord the letters of the missionaries in need, just like King Hezekiah did. I often cannot think of a solution myself. The circumstances are becoming so difficult. There is rebellion everywhere in China. We are experiencing more and more that there is resistance against the Christian faith. The missionaries in China are experiencing immense difficulties. And they expect an immediate answer to all their problems. But who am I?"

With a deep sigh Hudson sat down in one of the wicker chairs in the kitchen.

Maria quietly listened to her husband; she understood. Hudson was facing a difficult time. Everyone expected support and understanding from him. If possible, they even expected a solution to their problems, but that was not always possible.

"And you know what else, Maria? I am disappointed in myself every day. Lately my faith has been so weak. I look much more at my shortcomings than at the power of Him who governs and rules over this world."

"Unbelief is always sin, Hudson, but if we look at the last year it is understandable that you are so tired and worn out. We have gone through a lot. Think back to the great rebellion in Yangzhou. Do you still remember Saturday, August 22? Almost 10,000 people ran through the city howling. Thousands of people stood screaming in front of the house of the China Inland Mission. Sometimes when I'm in bed, it seems as if I can still hear their screaming voices, "Away with the Europeans! They are ruining our families. We may no longer honour our forefathers. The Chinese people may no longer be Chinese. Death to the Europeans!" You know how we and our children barely escaped death. I still cannot understand how I jumped down out of our bedroom window during our escape. I was six months pregnant with our little Charlie. It is a wonder that the child and I survived. In addition, we have the ongoing worries about Samuel's weak health. And despite all that, everyone expects to receive attention and advice from us. I don't think we can keep it up, can we?"

"It is true, Maria. The work is really getting to be too much. We are at the end of our strength. But ... where is my faith? I had hoped very much that our short stay on the island of Putuo this summer would give me renewed energy. But I am already at the end of my strength"

Maria put her arm around Hudson's shoulders. "You are also only a human being," she whispered. "You cannot continue endlessly working and helping others."

Discouraged, Hudson stared into the distance. How could he keep this up?

* * *

A few months later Hudson and Maria sat down together in the evening. They were tired from their busy day but thankful that God had helped them. It seemed as if Hudson's strength had been renewed in recent months. The Lord had greatly encouraged him with the words, "If we believe not, yet He abideth faithful." It had not lessened their worries about China, and also not about their children, but it seemed that the Lord was upholding them through their trials.

That evening they had laid out their plans before God and that gave them rest.

"It is the best solution that we can think of at the moment, Hudson. I agree that our four oldest children should leave for England in the spring. I will miss them a lot but the climate in England is much better for Herbert, Howard, Samuel and Maria. Also the irregular family life here in China and all the tensions they suffer are not good for them."

"I agree completely, Maria. I cannot stand the thought of not hearing those happy children's voices but, thankfully, we will still have our little Charlie with us."

* * *

August 2, 1870

Dear Mother,
　The Lord gave, and the Lord hath taken away; blessed be the name of the Lord.
　After our dear Samuel died this spring at the age of almost six years, the Lord took unto Himself our little Noel on July 20 and my dear wife Maria on July 23. She had contracted cholera shortly before the birth of Noel on July 7. The little boy only lived for thirteen days. He died from diarrhea and an infection. Maria was still able to choose a few hymns which we sang at his funeral. To her great sorrow, she was unable to attend the funeral because she was sick. She had internal bleeding and that caused her death in the end. Thankfully she suffered little pain but her strength declined daily.
　A few days before her death we received the message from Mrs. Berger from England that our children Herbert, Howard and Maria had arrived safely. That was a great comfort for Maria.
　It was deeply moving how she said farewell to all of us. She had a personal word for everyone. She also dictated a message for the children in England.
　When I saw her on Saturday morning, July 23, I noticed immediately that she was not doing well. She was very pale. We talked together about her imminent death. Her last words were, 'I am sad that I have to leave you alone at this difficult time, but I am going to the Lord.'
　After having been happily married to her for twelve and a half years, I had to say farewell to her. Six days after her death, the coffin was carried to the cemetery by eight Chinese men in white mourning clothes. All the missionaries, the British and American consuls, the foreign officers of the imperial custom house and almost all the English and American inhabitants of our area were at the cemetery. I told them about Maria's conversion and how God always took care of us. God knows the fruit of it.
　There is sorrow, but also joy. I find rest in the knowledge that God orders all things out of His Fatherly hand. He truly takes care that all things work together for good. He knows how much Maria meant to me, but He is closer by me than ever. And therefore, I say once more with Job, 'The Lord gave, and the Lord hath taken away; blessed be the name of the Lord.'

I commend you unto God,
Your son Hudson

25. The Eleventh and Last Trip

1871-1905

A large sailboat swayed back and forth slightly as it moved over the quiet sea between China and England. It was a warm summer day in 1871. Elizabeth Meadows was on the deck, enjoying her time with young Charlie Taylor who, along with his father, was on his way to visit his two brothers, Herbert and Howard, and his sister Maria, in England.

James Meadows, Elizabeth's husband, was sick in his cabin. The mission work in China had taken its toll on him. Therefore, they had decided to sail to London together with Hudson Taylor, Jenny Faulding, who was a teacher, and Li Fanfeng, a publisher.

While Elizabeth was enjoying her time with little Charlie Taylor, Hudson and Jenny retreated to a shady place on the other side of the ship. They had been together more often during the last few weeks. Hudson knew Jenny well. She had worked as a director of the schools in Hangzhou for five years. They had often talked together during the trip, but this time their conversation was not about their work ...

"I am really nothing without a wife," Hudson admitted. "It is now a year ago that Maria died, but I still miss her every day. I am so glad that soon I will be able to see my three children again. How I have longed for them during the past year."

"I understand, Hudson," Jenny nodded. "Maria was a very special woman. She was truly an unforgettable person. I loved her."

Hudson looked at Jenny in surprise. "So if your parents will give their permission for our marriage, will Maria also be in your thoughts?"

"I promise, Hudson. I will always remember her with respect and appreciation, and with much love."

"How thankful I am to you for that. Didn't I tell you that Maria's last wish was that I would remarry?"

"Yes, I knew that. Otherwise, I would not just have dared to say 'yes' when you asked me to share the rest of my life with you. The thought that it was Maria's wish makes it easier for me. Anyway, I am very curious how my parents will react. We have to ask for their permission, of course."

"I agree," Hudson nodded. "I hope that my age is not an objection for them. You are eleven years younger than me and you will have to take on the care of an entire family."

"That is not an objection for me, Hudson! If it is God's way, He will also give me what I need."

* * *

1904

It was thirty-two years later.

"Do you still remember …?" Jenny Taylor asked her husband as they were sitting in the garden, enjoying the view of the orange-red sun slowly disappearing behind the mountains. "Thirty-two years ago on the boat back to England we were worried whether my parents would give their permission for our marriage … Where has the time gone …?"

A soft smile shone on her face.

"It's true, Jenny," Hudson nodded. "Our life has flown by. Do you still remember how happy we were when we got married?"

"Were happy?" Jenny interrupted him. "I think we may say that we have always remained happy together. Looking back, I now wonder how I managed to take care of the children each time you were gone due to your work. It was sometimes a heavy task, but the Lord has always helped us."

She carefully wiped a few leaves off the pine table. "Do you know that I often think about the past lately?" she continued.

"I think it must have something to do with our age," Hudson answered. "I also frequently think of the past. And I won't deny that I left you by yourself many times. That sometimes makes me a little bit sad. But … I could not do anything different. The work for the China Inland Mission, and the work in China itself, grew by leaps and bounds during the past years. It kept me busy day and night. It took all my spare time. Well, I don't need to tell you that. You know that I first asked God for five missionaries, and later on for twenty-four. Since we got married we have together asked God for seventy workers, then for a hundred, and finally for a thousand people who wanted to spend their lives in the service of God's Kingdom. And each time God took care that we had the workers we asked for, even when we asked for a thousand of them! God has answered many prayers. All in all, because of our work, millions of people have heard the message of God's Word and salvation in Christ. We do not know what the fruit has been and we don't need to know that. God knows …"

Hudson and Jenny quietly stared into the distance for a minute.

Jenny was startled when Hudson suddenly broke the silence.

"Yes, it was special that we were allowed to do so much work in our short lives. But that does not mean that it was always easy to have to leave you with the children in England or China."

"Oh Hudson, I know. But you know that I completely agreed with what you did. You have never doubted that, have you?"

"Of course not! Your support really encouraged me. Also in difficult situations. I knew that you were at home, praying for me and our mission work. But I often had to leave you by yourself. Think about it: during the last thirty-two years I made eight trips to China. Sometimes by myself, but I'm glad you were able to come along on most of those trips."

"And what do you think of your trips to North America, Australia, New Zealand, Germany, Norway and Sweden?" Jenny said in a teasing voice. "I would have loved to come along when you were invited to go to Denmark for a private conversation with Queen Sophia."

"Yes, that's true," Hudson laughed. "I did go to Denmark. As far as that is concerned, we have not had much time for each other during our marriage. We are older now and I really enjoy relaxing and spending time with you in our own house on Lake Geneva. I have especially enjoyed going for walks through the mountains with you since we moved here in 1901. All in all, we may certainly say that

God has richly blessed us during the last thirty-two years. He has always cared for us, despite all the trials we faced. The devil tried everything to drive the Gospel out of China. Several times it even looked like everything that we had built up would be destroyed. Just think back to the year 1900, when the Boxer Rebellion broke out, causing such violence. Yes, that was definitely the lowest point! Fifty-eight adults and twenty-one children of the China Inland Mission lost their lives at that time. Do you remember? But God protected us. He even gave us more missionaries than we had asked for, from abroad as well as from China. The Gospel is proclaimed in many different places, even today."

Deep in thought they looked at the setting sun which shrouded the mountain tops in a red glow. Yes, they had often been deeply moved by the remarkable experiences of the last years.

"Hudson," Jenny said in a tired voice, "I think it's time to go inside. I am too tired to stay outside."

Anxiously Hudson looked at his wife. Jenny had become so thin recently! Thanks to his son Howard, Jenny had been put under anesthesia and examined by a well-known cancer doctor. They had diagnosed her with an internal tumour, but the specialist had advised that she should not be operated on. Hudson, however, kept worrying about her health.

A few weeks later, on July 29, 1904, the Lord took Jenny home. She calmly passed away with Hudson sitting by her bed.

* * *

1905

It was almost a year later ... Silence had returned to the Zhenjiang cemetery after the burial of Hudson Taylor's body.

That evening, Geraldine Taylor said to her husband in an emotional voice, "What a special day we had today, Howard. It was an impressive sight this morning to see the boat carrying your father's body slowly making its way down the Yangtze River. The coffin was the most expensive the Chinese Christians could afford! And the funeral itself was also very solemn."

"That's true, Geraldine. And what is special is that Father may now rest in this grave, along with my mother Maria, my two sisters and my two brothers, until the day that Jesus Christ will return."

"The last year of his life was a very difficult year for your father, Howard. After your second mother Jenny died, he often felt lonely. The two often talked together about the mission work in China. Many times your father needed to say only half a word before Jenny understood what he meant."

"That's true," Howard nodded. "Jenny was a loving wife! Father missed her terribly. Yet when we arrived in Shanghai with him on April 17, I did not think that his eleventh trip to China would also be his last."

"You are right," Geraldine agreed. "I had not expected that either. But God took him Home at His time. Your father's work in China is over. But God be praised, the mission work in China will continue because it is in God's hands!"

About the Author

While reading the last chapter, you might have wondered why the second part of Hudson Taylor's life was not described as extensively as the first. Did no miracles happen during the time that Hudson was married to his second wife Jenny? Oh, certainly! One example of a special miracle was when Hudson and Jenny, along with their workers, prayed for seventy workers and the Lord answered their prayers. Later on they prayed for one hundred workers and the Lord gave even more than one hundred workers who wanted to go to China. After that Hudson proposed during a conference that they should pray together for a thousand workers for the next five years. And do you know how many workers God gave them? They received 481 men and 672 women. A total of 1153 people! And not only that, but God also took care that there was enough money for all these people and for all the work of the China Inland Mission.

The reason why the choice was made to summarize the whole second period of Hudson's life in one chapter is that he made a lot of trips during that time. You can see a summary of his trips on pages 128-130. He went to China to give advice and to encourage people and, then, back to England. But he also travelled to other parts of the world and other countries in Europe to draw attention to the importance of mission work in China. So he was always busy for mission work in China but not just by evangelizing in China only. In addition, he often spoke at conferences.

This book speaks mainly about the time when Hudson was young. You have read how God led his life and, also, how the Lord did not forsake him when he wanted to forsake God. Everything he learned during his youth became of great benefit to him later on when he was a missionary. You have also read how mission work began in China. It was very difficult and there were a lot of difficulties to overcome. And yet ... God has used Hudson Taylor, along with the other workers, to bring the Gospel to millions of Chinese people, also in the interior. Is that not a wonder?

Hudson Taylor's Life

1832	James Hudson Taylor was born on May 21 in Barnsley, England.
1841	At age nine Hudson and Amelia often went to the woods with Father on Saturdays.
1843	At age eleven he went to school for the first time.
1845	At around age thirteen he worked for his father in the pharmacy.
1847-1849	From age fifteen until age seventeen he worked at the bank.
1849	Year of Hudson's conversion and calling.
1850	Hudson started to study Chinese. Doctor Robert Hardey offered him a place to stay.
1850-1864	Taiping Rebellion in China.
1851	In May, Hudson started to work for Doctor Hardey in Hull.
1852	Hudson began to live more frugally.
1852	After sixteen months with Doctor Hardey, Hudson started a specialized study in the eye hospital in London.
1853	On September 19, Hudson left for China for the first time. He was sent out by the Chinese Evangelization Society (CES).
1854	Arrival in Shanghai on March 1, 1854; from August 1 Hudson rented a house by himself.
1855	Hudson went to the Chinese interior with John Burdon and went to Tongzhou.
1855	Hudson dressed in Chinese clothing and adopted the Chinese hairstyle of wearing a braid.
1855	In December, Doctor Parker moved to Ningbo. Hudson rented a house in Shanghai and on the island of Chongming. He could only stay there for a few weeks.
1856	Along with missionary William Burns, Hudson left for a few months for Shantou or Swatow.
1856	Hudson returned to Shanghai for medicines. Everything had been destroyed by fire.
1856	Hudson left for Ningbo and worked in the hospital with Doctor Parker. He met Maria Dyer.
1857	Hudson handed in his resignation to CES.
1858	Hudson married Maria Dyer on January 20. At the end of October the little child that Maria was expecting died at childbirth.
1859	Rebellions in Ningbo; daughter Grace was born. Three weeks later, Hudson took over the responsibility of the hospital from Doctor Parker.
1860	Hudson was exhausted. He went to England with Maria and Grace. In England he and Maria prayed for five missionaries.

1860-1864	Hudson finished his medical studies and obtained a midwifery diploma. He translated the New Testament and some hymns into the Ningbo dialect. He gave lectures and wrote articles for magazines.
1865	Hudson surrendered to God on the beach of Brighton and prayed for twenty-four missionaries for China. The China Inland Mission was established.
1866	Hudson, Maria and their four children went to China for the second time. Sixteen helpers went along.
1867	Daughter Grace died from meningitis during the summer.
1868	Rebellion in Yangzhou.
1870	Samuel died in the spring. He was almost six years old.
1870	Noel died on July 20. He was thirteen days old.
1870	Maria died on July 23 at age 33.
1871	In August, Hudson travelled to England, along with Jenny Faulding and others. Hudson married Jenny on November 28.
1872	Hudson went to China for the third time with his wife Jenny.
1874	Hudson and Jenny returned to England.
1875	Hudson made an appeal for eighteen missionaries.
1876	Hudson went to China for the fourth time, without Jenny. He travelled with a group of female missionaries.
1877	Hudson arrived back in England in November.
1878	Hudson's wife Jenny travelled to China to assist orphans during a famine.
1878	Hudson travelled to Switzerland to recuperate from exhaustion.
1879	Hudson travelled to China for the fifth time.
1881	Jenny travelled to England where she stayed for nine years.
1881	Hudson prayed for seventy workers for China.
1883	Hudson arrived in England in February and was reunited with Jenny and his children.
1885	On January 20, Hudson left for China without his wife. It was his sixth trip to China.
1886	Hudson travelled through nine provinces from May till October.
1887	Hudson returned to England.
1888	Hudson travelled to North America with his son Howard and left from Vancouver for China with the first American missionaries.
1889	Hudson was back in England on May 21. In July he left again for North America. In November he visited Sweden, Norway and Denmark.
1890	In March, Hudson travelled to China for the eighth time. Jenny remained behind in England. That year he visited Australia for the first time.
1890	Hudson arrived in China on December 21. He travelled with Jenny who had not been in China for nine years.

1891	Many anti-foreign uprisings in China.
1892	Hudson was sick in Vancouver; he returned to England.
1893	Hudson visited Germany twice.
1894	Hudson went to China for the ninth time, this time via America, along with Jenny and daughter-in-law Geraldine.
1896	Hudson and Jenny left China in February because of sickness and returned to England. In March, Hudson visited India and in April, he returned to China. In May, he travelled to England, visiting Germany on the way. In August, he visited Sweden, Norway and Germany.
1897	Hudson went to southern France, then to Germany. In the summer he travelled to Switzerland with Jenny.
1897	In November, Hudson travelled to China for the tenth time, this time with Jenny.
1899	In the summer of that year the Boxer Rebellion started which caused a great uproar. In September, Hudson worked in China for the last time. On September 28, Hudson and Jenny left China for Australia and New Zealand. That was the end of Hudson's work in China.
1900	Hudson and Jenny visited New Zealand in January. In April, Hudson spoke at a conference in New York. In May, the Boxer Rebellion began in earnest. Hudson and Jenny arrived in England and continued on to Switzerland.
1901	Hudson and Jenny bought a house on Lake Geneva.
1904	Jenny died on July 30 and was buried in Switzerland.
1905	In the spring, Hudson left for China with his son Howard and his daughter-in-law Geraldine. It was his eleventh and last trip to China. Hudson died on July 3 in Changsha at the age of 73. He was buried in Zhenjiang.

Important People in this Book

Hudson Taylor's family:

James Taylor	Hudson Taylor's father	1807-1881
Amelia Hudson Taylor	Hudson Taylor's mother	1808-1881
James Hudson Taylor	Main character of this book	1832-1905
William Taylor	Hudson Taylor's brother who died young	1834-1841
Amelia Taylor	Hudson Taylor's younger sister	1835
Louisa Taylor	Hudson Taylor's youngest sister	1840
Benjamin Broomhall	Amelia's husband	

Hudson Taylor's Relatives:

Aunt Hannah Hudson	Sister of Hudson's mother who lived in Barton-upon-Humber
John (cousin)	Son of Aunt Hannah of Barton-on-Humber
Aunt Hannah Hardey	Hudson's aunt, who lived in Hull and had no children
Uncle Richard Hardey	Photographer, husband of Aunt Hannah from Hull
Benjamin Hudson	Hudson's uncle, brother of his mother, lived in London
Tom Hudson	Hudson's cousin, brother of cousin John, lived in London

Doctors, friends and others with whom Hudson had contact in England:

William Berger	Man who initially donated much money for mission work in China. Later on he was instrumental in establishing the China Inland Mission (CIM)
Doctor Brown	Surgeon in London
Doctor Clarke	Former professor, later on doctor in London who treated Hudson
Captain Finch	Husband of Mrs. Finch, from whom Hudson rented a room in Drainside
Doctor Robert Hardey	Surgeon in Hull, brother-in-law of Aunt Hannah
John Puget	Colonel who met Hudson when he was back in England
Rev. Plunkett	Old minister from Liverpool
Elizabeth Sissons	Friend of Amelia

| Arthur Taylor | Friend, who was also sent to China as a missionary after Hudson |
| Marianne Vaughan | Friend of Amelia. Hudson dated her for three years and was engaged to her |

Doctors, friends and others with whom Hudson worked in China:

Mrs. Aldersey	Head mistress of the first girls school in China
John Burdon	English minister in Shanghai
William Burns	Older missionary with whom Hudson visited the interior
Burella Dyer	Teacher in Ningbo, sister of Maria Dyer
Maria Dyer	Teacher in Ningbo, Hudson's first wife
Frederick Gough	English missionary in China, helped to translate the New Testament into the dialect of Ningbo
John Jones	English missionary, also sent out by the CES
Mary Jones	Wife of John Jones
Doctor William Lockhart	Doctor who founded a hospital in Shanghai
Doctor Medhurst	One of the most important missionaries from England in China
James and Martha Meadows	Missionary couple who left England to go to China
Elizabeth Meadows	English missionary, second wife of James Meadows. She worked in China
Jean Norman	English missionary who was sent to China
Doctor William Parker	Doctor in Shanghai, later hospital doctor in Ningbo
Captain Bowers	Christian Captain whom Hudson met in Shanghai
Captain Morris	Captain of the sailboat Dumfries

Family of first marriage of Hudson Taylor to Maria Dyer; married in January 1858

Maria Hudson Dyer	First wife of Hudson, died at age 33 1837-1870 After a pregnancy of seven months October 1858 their first baby died
Grace Dyer Hudson	Oldest daughter of Hudson and Maria, 1859-1867 died at age eight
Herbert Hudson	Oldest son of Hudson and Maria 1861
Frederick Howard	Second son 1862
Geraldine Taylor	Daughter-in-law; she married Frederick Howard
Samuel	Third son, died when he was almost six 1865-1870
Maria Hudson	Second daughter 1867
Noel	Fourth son, lived for only thirteen days 1870-1870

Second marriage of Hudson Taylor to Jenny Faulding, married November 1871

    Jenny Taylor Faulding   Second wife of Hudson, died at age 61   1843-1904

Organisations based in England which worked in China:

Chinese Evangelization Society (CES)
China Inland Mission (CIM)

| Charles Bird | Secretary of Chinese Evangelization Society (CES) |
| George Pearce | Secretary of China organization, later co-founder of the China Inland Mission |